Stop Lying to Yourself

Why Everything You've Tried Hasn't Changed You

Dr. Lester Clowes

DEFY Press

Disclaimer

This book is intended for general informational and educational purposes only. It reflects the author's own experience and opinions as a performance coach. It is not a substitute for the advice, diagnosis, or treatment of a qualified medical or mental health professional. Nor should it replace the counsel of a legal, financial, or other professional.

Reading this book does not create a coaching, therapeutic, or other professional relationship between you and the author. If you have concerns about your physical or mental health, consult a licensed physician, therapist, or other qualified provider. Never disregard professional advice or delay seeking it because of something you have read here. If you are in crisis or may be a danger to yourself or others, contact a licensed professional or your local emergency services right away.

The author and publisher make no guarantee that the ideas or practices in this book will produce any particular result, and individual results will vary. To the fullest extent permitted by law, the author and publisher disclaim any liability for loss, risk, or harm claimed to result from the use or application of any content in this book.

All formats

Hardcover | ISBN: 979-8-9952824-2-6

Paperback | ISBN: 979-8-9952824-0-2

Ebook | ISBN: 979-8-9952824-3-3

Contents

Acknowledgements

"Believe in the me that believes in you."

— Kamina, *Gurren Lagann*

To Pennee. You are the Kamina to my Simon. Just, please don't die fighting any mechs. Without your unwavering confidence in me, I would have nothing.

To Kiera and Chloe. Our writing hours together are what kept me on this journey. Now you need to finish your own books. Beat you to it.

To Amy B. You were a unicorn long before your brother started telling the world about it. Without your energy and critical feedback, I would have settled for a final draft short of what this book was capable of.

To Bobo. Like magic, any time my energy is running low or I'm feeling in a rut, we end up on a call talking for hours. Dare to Dad forever.

To Rhonda Byrne. I still think The Secret is one of the worst self-help books ever written. But my wife read it and she kicked my ass into starting my own coaching practice. So maybe there's something there.

Introduction: You've Been Doing This Backwards.

It was January. First day back from winter break and I was a school leader at the time. Live video call. Cameras on. And that's when the executive team announced they'd created the VP role I'd been promised first shot at... And filled it. No heads-up or warning of any kind. Just a real-time gut-punch in front of a hundred of my peers, many of whom knew exactly what was happening to me.

I wasn't always a life coach with a waiting list of clients. For years, I was one who needed the coaching and mentoring. Stuck in the exact patterns this book dismantles, consuming the same content I now argue against, and lying to myself with the same fluency I see in the people who sit across from me today.

More than 9,000 hours of one-on-one coaching sessions will teach you a few things. You don't need more motivation. You need better operating systems. You don't need inspiration. You need disruption. And you sure as hell don't need another guru promising easy, life-changing transformations.

What you're holding is a collection of hard-earned truths that could collapse the gap between who you're pretending to be and who you actually are. You've built an identity on self-deception, excuses, and broken promises, and you've been lying to yourself about it for so long you've stopped noticing. That's why this book was written.

The Zombie Years

For six years, I had poured everything into an organization I helped grow from one small school on the beach to a national powerhouse. My identity was the organization, and it was me. Culture builder. Systems creator. The leader with perfect feedback scores who built the hiring processes, helped write the organizational wiki, and served on nearly every action team fighting fire after fire.

Then came the promised career-defining opportunity that, well, kind of never materialized. Instead, my talents and personality had shifted from asset to liability, and they filled the role behind my back.

I stayed another two and a half years, but as a zombie. The high-performing leader was gone. I became the guy who had once led the charge, now checking out at 4:59PM with nothing left to give. Showing up but never present. Collecting more accolades but feeling nothing.

But this sense of self inevitably bled into other areas of my life. When you've given up control, that core identity isn't a switch you can cut on and off at will. So I was hollow at home, too. The man my family loved was still in the house, but I was gone. Not tired. Not burned out. Just gone.

That's when I found the drug of choice for smart, ambitious people who feel lost... Motivation porn.

Books about billionaire mindsets. Podcasts promising breakthrough frameworks. Online courses that felt like progress. Constant scrolling of curated social feeds full of motivational influencers whose only success was selling the illusion of success. I even spent my vacation time (yes, my actual vacation time) going to self-development conferences.

I was completely addicted to motivation porn. The constant temporary hits of inspiration that felt like momentum but changed nothing. The illusion of progress without the inconvenience of actual work.

Sunday night, I was a bald Tony Robbins. Monday morning, I was fired up and ready to change the world. Monday night? Back in the exact same loop. Same job and grind. Same disconnected self.

Motivation porn has one goal, and that's to keep you consuming. Because the moment you legitimately transform your life, you stop needing their next hit.

This is why this book works differently. Instead of giving you more to consume, it's going to make you uncomfortable. Every chapter names a lie you've been telling yourself, and then demands you do something about it. My job is to make it impossible for you to ignore why you are where you are today.

The Mirror Moment

For two and a half years I had a routine. Come home, see Pennee and the girls for a few minutes, then disappear into my office. I told them I was building something. I told myself the same thing.

What was really happening in that office? I was doing what I did at work... Performing. Scrolling for inspiring quotes. Signing up for another course I'd never finish. Maybe reading three pages of a book before the tab-switching started. And eventually, when the inspiration dried up, playing video games. Every night I'd close the laptop or book feeling like I'd made progress, when in reality I hadn't moved a single inch.

I didn't hear my daughter come in one night. She was five, and I swear to god she has ninja blood in her. She stood off to my right (of course I had my monitor turned away from the door) and saw what was on my screen, which was Hearthstone (video game, card battling). I watched her face fall when she figured it out. And I tried to explain it away, but she didn't want to hear it. She was five years old and she was always sharp, and she knew I was lying.

Pennee knew too. She'd known for a long time, but was patiently giving me space to figure myself out. Years of space. Yes, I don't deserve her.

So one night, she finally said it. "When are you going to stop moping? You can either stay there and keep dying, or you can quit and bet on yourself. Me and the girls believe in you. Believe in yourself." It might have knocked the wind out of me, but at least she was the only person in my life still willing to tell me the truth. And I'll forever be grateful for her courage.

Yes, the person who kicked my ass into motion was my wife. Not a motivational video or bestselling book. She might kill me for saying this but she's read one self-development book her whole life, and it's one of the worst ever published.

I went into my garage that night and sat in the dark. I wish I could say it was to reflect, but nope. I was hiding from the fact that I was living as the one thing I claimed to despise. A coward. I'd had it pounded into me growing up that great things were for other people, that playing it safe was wisdom, that wanting too much was how you got embarrassed. And somehow, despite a doctorate, despite being the first in my family to leave my hometown, despite helping build an organization from one school to fifty... I still believed it. Some part of me had always believed it.

I had to sit with one question that night. Was the Lester who built all of that actually real? Or had that all been performance too?

I eventually left the garage with the early framing for what I'd come to call Promise Debt. My self-reputation had bottomed out, and I could feel it. My personal record was a wreck and so was my read on my own word. But I wrote a few small promises to keep to myself that next morning, and I began the journey that has led me to you.

It wasn't a "find yourself" seminar led by an internet guru to the tune of $5K. It was my wife telling me the truth when I'd lost the ability to tell it to myself. And that was the best thing that ever happened to me.

I wrote this book to do the same for you.

From Breakdown to DEFY

Within six weeks of walking away, I had my first handful of paying coaching clients. I'd been forced to figure out what worked versus what just felt good, and even the people around me could feel and see the difference.

The first seven years of my practice became the laboratory where DEFY was forged, where I learned to help people reset their mindset, redesign their systems, and reclaim their future. Every person who walked through my door was tired of accepting average. They wanted to DEFY the life they'd settled for and build something that mattered.

And along the way, I discovered that lost people stay stuck because they've never learned how to systematically deconstruct the lies they tell themselves and replace them with frameworks that work.

Every method in this book was tested on me first, then refined with people who refused to accept that "this is just how it is." DEFY is what survived after everything that only sounded good got stripped away.

What Is Identity?

Identity is the backbone of this whole book, so let's be sure we're on the same page before we continue on. Most people get identity all wrong, which is exactly why they can't change it. You can't rebuild something you can't define.

Your identity is the sum of a few things stacked on top of each other. Your core beliefs about yourself and the world. The way you see yourself. The perspective you bring to whatever happens to you. The values that drive your decision-making. And then, sitting on top of all of it, your habits and routines... The things you do on a random Tuesday when no one else is around to influence you.

That top layer (habits) is the one everybody obsesses over, mistaking it for the whole machine. But your habits aren't the identity. They're the output. They're what the layers underneath have been quietly producing the whole time. The guy checking out at 4:59 with nothing left to give wasn't lazy. His behavior was an honest printout of beliefs he'd stopped examining.

Most of the time, that runs one direction. Your beliefs set the terms, your behavior obeys, and the behavior loops back to confirm the belief that started it. We'll call it the behavior loop for the rest of the book. Believe you're someone who can't finish what they start, and you'll half-ass it, walk away, and collect fresh proof you were right. It's why so many people sit and wait to feel different before they'll act different. They're standing outside their own beliefs, waiting to feel capable before they'll act capable. Waiting for permission that never comes. You cannot simply decide to believe you're capable. Try it. Sit there and order yourself to believe it. Nothing happens. (That's all an affirmation is, and it's why they fail the people who need them most.)

But the next move is still yours. You don't get to choose what you believe this morning, but you do get to choose whether you make the bed. And every time you do the thing that contradicts the old story, you hand the belief layer a piece of evidence it can't argue with. Stack enough of those moments over enough days, and the beliefs upstream finally update to match. You out-prove the old story instead of trying to argue yourself into a new one.

This isn't a reframe I cooked up to sound clever. When researchers took one of the most respected treatments for depression and stripped it down to only the behavioral part, cutting out the work on thoughts entirely, the behavior-only version worked just as well as the full package. You change what you do, and the rest of you eventually catches up. That's the whole backbone of this book. I'm not here to fix your thinking so you can finally act. I'm here to change what you do until your thinking has no choice but to follow. (I've put the studies in the back, for the receipt-checkers. As well as some acknowledgments to my favorite reads and frameworks from others. No tiny numbers cluttering your read.)

And the loop doesn't care which story it feeds. It confirms whatever you keep proving, and for most people, it's spent years confirming the wrong one.

You feel like you've done everything right and you still feel hollow. You know something's off but you can't quite name it. I've heard some form of that across thousands of coaching conversations, and almost every time the same thing was underneath it. You've been breaking promises to yourself for so long that you've stopped believing your own word. That's Promise Debt. Every broken commitment to yourself is a withdrawal from your self-reputation, and the felt cost is self-trust. This book is about paying that debt down the only way it comes down, one kept promise at a time, until the ledger is rebuilt and the belief comes back with it.

How to Use This Book (And Why Most People Get It Wrong)

You're going to want to apply all 18 lessons. That's the first trap, because wanting isn't winning. And reading isn't transformation.

Real change happens when you pick 1-3 lessons that punch you in the gut, that make you think "holy shit, that's exactly what I needed to hear," and then you live them until they become part of who you are.

Not part of what you know. Part of who you are.

Every chapter holds actions to take and ways to practice what you've learned. They're your bridge between reading and becoming, so don't treat them as suggestions. Most people will skip these. Don't be most people.

And track evidence, not intentions. Your journal should be full of what you truthfully did. And when something feels uncomfortable, that's your growth edge. Lean into it.

You'll feel resistance. You'll want to quit. You'll tell yourself stories about why this particular lesson doesn't apply to your unique situation. **Don't listen. That's your comfort zone negotiating for its life.**

But the most dangerous thing about this book is what it will ask you to stop being. It will challenge your identity, your excuses, and the carefully constructed reasons you have for staying exactly where you are. Some of you aren't ready for that level of honesty, and that's fine. There are thousands of other books that will make you feel better without asking you to change.

But if you're tired of playing small, tired of making excuses, tired of living a life that feels like a rough draft of what you really want... Then keep reading.

PART 1: IDENTITY DESTRUCTION

MINI: You Can't Vision Board a Six-Pack.

Let me paint you a picture that would be hilarious if it weren't so common.

Walk into any Target or Barnes & Noble and you'll find an entire aisle dedicated to a very common delusion, the belief that wanting something badly enough is the same as earning it. Vision board kits. Manifestation journals. "Dream it, believe it, achieve it" planners with enough positive affirmations to choke a life coach.

Someone cuts out photos of shredded abs from fitness magazines, and then pastes them on a vision board next to quotes about "believing in yourself" and "manifesting your best body." They light a candle, sit in front of their masterpiece, and visualize having a six-pack.

Then they order DoorDash and skip the gym.

Or buy an awesome new set of gym clothes. That then never see a drop of actual sweat.

Again. Just like they did after last year's resolutions... Or last week.

You're laughing because you know this person. Hell, you might *be* this person. And deep down, you know how ridiculous it sounds to think you can "Pinterest" your way to fitness.

So why do you think you can vision board your way to everything else? Just admit it... You're not manifesting. You're procrastinating. Designing instead of building, and planning instead of doing. You're visualizing instead of showing up.

But beautiful plans don't change broken patterns.

I can't tell you how many people show up to their first coaching sessions with me, with these gorgeous goal-setting frameworks and color-coded calendars that belong in a productivity magazine. They've got vision boards that look like art projects and planning systems that would make a project manager weep with joy.

And they're stuck in exactly the same place they were four months ago... Or even four years ago.

They've confused aesthetics with effort. And they've mistaken clarity for action. They've made planning a performance, and convinced themselves it counts. But I want you to understand that great abs are earned in sweat, not software. Every time you choose the stairs over the elevator or water over soda, that's what builds the body you want. Not the vision board. Not the perfectly curated Instagram feed of fitness motivation.

Perfection doesn't prove commitment. Execution does. The work. The boring, unglamorous, no-one's-watching work.

This applies to everything else you've been trying to manifest instead of build. That business you've been vision boarding for two years? It needs customers, not collages. The relationship you want? Communication skills matter more than candles and crystals. Your dream promotion will show up when your performance does.

Your bank account doesn't care how many times you wrote "abundance" in your journal. And that novel you've been "working on"? The deadline isn't going to set itself. You want to meet successful people? Stop collecting their headshots and start showing up where they actually hang out.

Stop designing your future and start building it. Brick by brick.

Stop collecting proof of other people's success. Start creating your own, starting however small it takes to create real momentum.

Stop trying to manifest change, as if the universe owes you something. Start manufacturing it for yourself, one rep, one choice, one uncomfortable action at a time.

Motivation gets you started, but systems get you through. The right system keeps running when motivation doesn't show up and you don't feel like moving. And it leaves you with something a vision board never will... Proof you did the work.

The vision board industry has convinced you that clarity equals progress. **But clarity without action is just expensive procrastination.** The person with a clear vision and no execution plan is still exactly where they started, just with better wall decorations.

Real transformation happens in the gap between what you said you'd do and what you truly do. You earn it by choosing the hard option because it's the right one, and acting like the person you want to become before you feel like them.

You don't need another picture of success. You need to become one.

CHALLENGE

Take that goal you've been vision-boarding or manifesting. Now write down one action that would move you toward it, right now. Not tomorrow. Something you could do in the next hour, and something that requires effort. Not just something that might look impressive on your Instagram feed in a selfie.

Make it specific. Make it measurable. Make it uncomfortable enough that your brain will try to talk you out of it.

Then stop reading and go do it. Right now. Before you check your phone or make a coffee, or do anything else that feels like progress but isn't.

Because you can't vision board a six-pack. But you can earn one.

And the same goes for everything else you want in this life.

Chapter 1

You've Mistaken Comfort for Progress.

THE LIE: You want a different life, and you've really tried for one. So the problem has to be your circumstances, since it certainly isn't you. Change what's around you and you'll finally close the gap.
WHY IT HOLDS: Because some of what's held you back really wasn't your fault, and that part is true enough to let you off the hook. But the jobs changed, the cities changed, the relationships changed, and you ended up in the same place every time. At some point, the only constant left is you.

You're stuck.

Maybe you won't admit it to others, but you know it. Same income for three years. Same arguments with your partner. Same twenty pounds you can't seem to lose. Same promises you make every Sunday night and break by Wednesday morning.

The promotion conversations that go nowhere, even though you know you're qualified. The business idea that's been sitting in your notes app for two years. The relationship patterns that repeat like clockwork. Different person, same problems. The health goals that reset every January and die by February.

And I get it. It's not like you haven't tried. You've done the readings and listened to the experts. Who knows, you might have even paid for one of those weekend seminars that promised to be the event that would "change your life forever."

But nothing changed.

You're still here, wanting the same things you wanted last year. Still looking at the same gap between what you have and what you want.

Because nothing changes if nothing changes.

Hoping Isn't Changing

You probably went to bed with good intentions. But then you hit snooze. Again. Then told yourself tomorrow would be different. Scrolled on your phone for twenty minutes before your feet hit the floor. Then you made the same choices you made yesterday. Comfortable but not healthy breakfast. Put off important conversations by actively avoiding text messages. Each choice made with a perfectly reasonable explanation for why today wasn't the day to start becoming someone different.

You told yourself you'd speak up in that meeting, but you stayed quiet. You'd have the difficult conversation with your parents, but the timing wasn't quite right. You'd finally commit to the morning workout routine, but you're in the middle of a busy season at work.

Sound familiar?

This is comfort with a better view in action. You want the life that comes from being disciplined, courageous, and consistent. But you're not willing to become the person who is those things. You want the outcomes without the identity shift.

You scroll LinkedIn and feel inspired by people building businesses, then you close the app and do nothing. You listen to podcasts about high performers, then you spend your evening exactly the same way you spent last evening. You read books about transformation, then you stay exactly the same person who started reading. You've convinced yourself that consuming information about change is the same as truly changing. That planning to be different is the same as being different. That wanting better is the same as doing better.

It's not.

If you want to achieve something you've never had before, you must become someone you've never been before. Someone fundamentally different in how you think, act, and show up in the world. That's the truth most aren't willing to confront. And I see this constantly with clients (and potential clients). They will speak to wanting meaningful change, but all they're really willing to work for is comfort with a better view.

They want the promotion without the discomfort of creating massive value for their organization with no guaranteed return on their investment. In other words, they want different outcomes while remaining exactly the same person.

The Comfort You're Actually Choosing

Let's get specific about what you're prioritizing when you choose comfort over change.

You're choosing the comfort of not risking failure over the possibility of real success. It's safer to stay qualified-but-overlooked than to become someone who demands recognition through undeniable value creation.

You're choosing the comfort of familiar relationship patterns over the vulnerability of actual intimacy. It's easier to keep having surface-level connections than to risk being fully seen and possibly rejected, so you allow your relationships to exist within stuck patterns of guardedness and avoidance.

You can explain why you're stuck. You have reasons. Valid ones. But those reasons are keeping you exactly where you are, so you never pursue the discomfort of excellence.

Who you are right now is known. This identity is safe. Predictable. Even if it's not working, at least it's familiar. The idea of building a new identity carries far too much risk, so you settle for your current one with all of its inherent limitations.

But the promotion you want requires you to become someone who creates value beyond your job description, who builds relationships that influence outcomes, who demonstrates leadership before you're given the title. But that's uncomfortable. It doesn't come with any guarantees.

The relationship you want requires you to become someone who can handle conflict without shutting down, who can express needs without becoming needy, who can be intimate without losing yourself. But that's vulnerable, and that's freaking scary.

The body you want requires you to become someone who chooses discipline over convenience, who prioritizes long-term health over short-term comfort, who shows up even when motivation is gone. But that's hard. And you have a long history of giving up on hard things.

So you settle for comfort with a better view. You want to see yourself as someone who's trying, who has potential, who's going to change... Eventually. You just don't want to do the uncomfortable work of changing right now.

But the world doesn't work that way. It never has.

Your life right now is a perfect reflection of who you currently are. Not who you want to be, not who you could be, but who you are right now. Your relationships, your bank account, your health, your career trajectory. All of it is evidence of the person you've been willing to become so far. Who you've been willing to sacrifice for. To build for.

That reflection is the behavior loop from the introduction, still reinforcing the only story you've ever allowed yourself to tell. Every comfortable choice hands the old identity another piece of evidence that it's correct... That this is who you are, and who you'll stay. Choosing comfort is an active deposit on the person you keep saying you want to grow *away from*. Your brain keeps score with behavior, and your behavior has been confirming the old story every single day you've waited to feel different.

And until that person changes, your life won't either.

Performing the Identity

I lived this pattern for years before I could put a name to it. I wanted to be someone who wrote books, a real author. I even had over a million words of written content across half-finished manuscripts and abandoned ideas. In the various moments of putting pen to paper, it felt like progress. At times it even felt like real momentum. But every time it came to actually finishing something (committing to the ending, closing the loop) I found a reason to start over. Better idea. Wrong angle. But I knew what was really happening. I was performing the identity of a writer without becoming one. It wasn't until I got honest about who I needed to be, and then built a process around that person, that I finally finished this book you're holding in your hands. That pattern shows up everywhere. In careers. In relationships. In the people who sit across from me every week.

If you're already thinking "This doesn't apply to me," you're wrong. Marcus thought the same thing. Top performer. Consistently hitting goals. But still feeling completely stuck with himself professionally. And the problem wasn't his circumstances. It was him.

"No one takes me seriously," he told me during our first call. "I've been the top rep for three years running, but they won't promote me. I can't even get an invite to strategy meetings. I'm doing everything right, but I'm getting nowhere."

Marcus wanted tactics. He wanted to know how to demand respect, how to position himself for leadership, how to make his executive team finally recognize his value. Instead, I asked him a question he wasn't ready to confront, but I owed him.

"What if the problem isn't that they don't see your value? What if the problem is that you're not YET the person who can handle the promotion and responsibilities you're asking for?"

He didn't like that question. But he was at least desperate enough to consider it.

Within weeks, the truth emerged. Marcus operated like a lone wolf. He hoarded information and tactics because he didn't want others to beat him on the leaderboards, or he believed it was a waste of time since they couldn't do what he could anyway. He was defensive in meetings and quick to point out why other people's ideas wouldn't work. He treated every interaction like a competition he had to win rather than a collaboration where he could contribute.

Marcus wanted to be seen as leadership material, but he was behaving like someone who couldn't be trusted with a team. He wasn't creating space for others to contribute. He wasn't demonstrating the emotional intelligence that real leadership requires, or building the relationships that could influence others to follow him. He was proving, every day, that he wasn't ready for this next step he was demanding.

The work wasn't about learning new tactics. He had tried all the hacks, but they never touched the real problem. Marcus had to become someone who could handle what he was asking for. So we rolled up our sleeves and got to work rebuilding his identity from the ground up. Most importantly, Marcus was willing to do what it took. He could see that change was worth the discomfort.

Six months later, his boss pulled him aside and said, "We've been watching, and you've changed. The whole team feels it." He had become a topic in those strategy meetings he was never invited to, and in the end Marcus didn't have to "fight" for his promotion. Instead, he'd earned it by becoming someone who could handle this new level of responsibility.

I've seen this same dynamic in moms returning to the workforce, athletes hitting mental blocks, and even teenagers applying to college. Stuck shows up everywhere. But the path out? It always begins the same... Identity first.

And you might recognize yourself in Marcus's story. That means you're seeing the patterns you've been avoiding. Most people will close this book right here because confronting who they truly are is scarier than staying stuck.

Don't be most people.

The identity-first approach requires admitting something painful, that the problem isn't your circumstances, your luck, or other people. The problem is who you've been willing to become so far. Coaching hundreds of people through this process has taught me a critical lesson. The moment you stop trying to fix your circumstances and start rebuilding your identity, growth starts to feel real and earned. The problems in life won't shrink. They never will. But you can outgrow them.

You have the power to own where you are right now, AND you can refuse to stay there.

Standing Still Is Moving Backwards

Before we talk about how to change, let's get real about what happens when you don't.

Every day you stay stuck compounds in the wrong direction. That income plateau is bigger than this year's earnings. It's the raises you won't get, the opportunities you won't be considered for, the confidence you won't build. Staying the same person who got you here guarantees you'll still be here in five years... Except older and more frustrated.

The relationship patterns you're tired of? They're training the people in your life to expect less from you, and to work around your limitations instead of depending on your strengths. Every time you show up unchanged, you're teaching others that change isn't really possible for you.

Even worse? While you're maintaining your comfort zone, so many others around you are growing. Your colleagues are being promoted ahead of you. Your friends are solving problems you're still complaining about. The gap between who you could be and who you're choosing to be gets wider... Every. Single. Day.

Think about it mathematically. If you improve a small amount each month and your peers improve significantly more, the distance between you compounds exponentially. After one year, they're in a completely different category. They're having conversations you can't contribute to, solving problems you can't handle, and living lives you can't access.

The cost of staying the same is becoming someone you wouldn't choose to follow. Not at work. Not at home. Not even in your own damn mirror. And once you lose respect for yourself, you lose the ability to believe change is possible.

The Mirror Never Lies

To begin moving forward, you must accept that your life is a mirror, reflecting exactly who you are right now. And that mirror doesn't lie, even when you wish it would. This mirror operates in every area of your life, showing you exactly who you've been willing to become so far. It doesn't care about your intentions. It doesn't care about your potential. It only reflects your actual choices, day after day, year after year.

I know what it feels like to face that mirror and avoid all eye contact with yourself, living full of shame and regret. My oldest daughter was five when she picked out a Captain America shirt for me. We have a mutual love of anime and comics, so it was her idea because she saw me as her superhero. It even had "All-Star Dad" printed across the chest. I put it on and felt like a fraud... Because I was one. Every night I'd come home and spend a few minutes with my family, then flee to my office. I was performing the idea of building something. For my future. For their future. But I was really only hiding from hard truths. My daughter believed I was her hero, and instead her hero was faking progress and playing video games. The mirror doesn't care about the gap between who you are and who you want to be. It shows you both truths.

You don't get what you want. You get who you are.

That cluttered desk? You tell yourself it's because you're busy, but it's really because you don't value clarity. The gym membership collecting dust? You blame time constraints, but you don't prioritize your wellbeing. Those half-finished projects? Not perfectionism. You're someone who starts things and doesn't finish them.

Your calendar tells the most honest story of all. It shows your actual priorities, not what you claim is important. Look at last week. How many hours went to the thing you say is most important to you? How much of your Saturday protected the relationship you claim to be investing in? Did the people who matter most get your best hours... Or your leftover ones? The question isn't whether you mean well. The question is whether anyone following your schedule would recognize that.

The mirror shows you everything you need to know about who you really are right now. But are you willing to look?

Get Honest First

Before you can change anything, you have to first get very honest about where you are right now. Not the version of you presented on social media for the world to see. Not the person you tell others you're in the process of becoming. But the actual you. With all the patterns, defaults, and contradictions.

I still have the Captain America shirt, by the way. Ten years and twenty pounds of muscle later, it's more spandex than cotton (and my wife has banned it from public appearances). But I still wear it around the house. Sure, it makes a great dad joke. But one day I put it on and realized I was smiling. Not avoiding eye contact with myself. Just... Smiling. The shirt felt earned. Not from a single moment of transformation, not from one big decision or breakthrough. But from breakfast made every morning. From school pickups built into the calendar like they were non-negotiable, because they were. From monthly dates with my girls that didn't get moved for anything in the world. The shirt didn't change. I did. And one day the mirror agreed.

Nothing changes if nothing changes. But the moment you're willing to change (really change, at the identity level) the rest of this book becomes a blueprint instead of a mirror.

Not easy. Not immediate. But possible.

If you want to achieve something you've never had before, you must become someone you've never been before.

CHALLENGE

You can't change what you refuse to confront. It's time to get brutally honest about who you are versus who you think you are.

Step 1: The Evidence Review. Look at your last three months. Write down what your REAL behavior proves about your identity in these areas:

- Money (What does your spending reveal about your values?)
- Health (What do your daily choices say about your priorities?)
- Relationships (How do you show up when it matters?)

- Work (What does your performance prove about your character?)

Step 2: The Gap Analysis. For each area, ask yourself:

- Who am I currently being? Who am I right now?
- Who do I need to become to get the results I want?
- What's the biggest gap between these two identities?

Step 3: Choose Your Identity. Pick ONE area where the gap is costing you the most, and then write down:

- The specific identity you need to develop.
- Three behaviors this new identity would demonstrate daily.
- One micro-commitment you can make today to start becoming this person.

Don't try to fix everything at once. Pick one identity shift and live it for 30 days until it becomes part of who you are.

Remember that you don't get what you want. You get who you are.

The Truth

You haven't been waiting on better circumstances. You've been waiting on a version of yourself you haven't built yet.

Your life right now is a mirror. And mirrors don't lie... Even when you wish they would.

You can't want your way into a different life. The person who has what you want isn't who you are right now. That's not an insult, it's the only honest starting point.

If this one hit hard: Chapter 17 (The Last Lie) is where the exhaustion underneath the comfort finally gets named. Not as a diagnosis, as a recognition. Chapter 12 (This Is Where You Always Quit) is where the work of building something different begins.

Hold On...

You just read Chapter 1's challenge. The Identity Audit. Did you do it? Or did you read it, nod, and keep moving?

Be honest. (You already know.)

Most people skip it. They tell themselves they'll come back once they've read a little more, maybe gotten the full picture or built some momentum first. But they won't. The reading feels like progress, so the doing keeps getting pushed to later. That gap, between knowing and doing, is the entire thing this book is about.

The challenges are the work. The chapters are just the argument for why you should finally do it.

So before you turn the page, go back and actually do the audit. Then meet me in Chapter 2.

Chapter 2

You're Not a Victim of Your Perspective. You're the Author.

THE LIE: You're a realist. You're not being negative, you're just seeing the situation for what it actually is. Anyone in your position would see it this way.
WHY IT HOLDS: Because it's partially true. Your history did shape how you see. But "shaped by" and "controlled by" aren't the same thing. And most people never notice the difference.

In Chapter 1, we talked about becoming someone new. But before you get too deeply into changing who you are, you also need to change how you see. Because your perspective shapes more than your thoughts, it constructs the reality you live within.

Almost everyone will experience *that* moment of clarity. They'll see themselves honestly and mean it when they say something has to change. And then, within hours or days, the narration starts. The internal voice that explains away what they saw, and then quietly negotiates them back to the comfortable. That voice isn't random noise, it's perspective... The lens through which you assign meaning to everything, including what you just saw in the mirror. And if you don't learn to choose that lens deliberately, it will choose for you. Every time.

Most people don't live. They react.

They wake up, check their phone, and immediately start responding to everyone else's agenda. Bad traffic? Their day is ruined. Critical feedback? They're a failure. Market downturn? They panic.

And all day long, they bounce from circumstance to circumstance like a pinball, ricocheting off whatever life throws at them while never pausing to realize they've surrendered all their power to external influences. The few who don't react?

They've figured out what everyone else refuses to accept. You're not a victim of your circumstances. You're the author of your response to them.

Almost no event (past or present) arrives with a fixed meaning. You either allow the meaning to be assigned *to you*, or *you determine* the meaning yourself. This is why two people can witness the same event unfold, with one walking away and their life forever changed and the other carrying on as if nothing occurred.

Your perspective is the editor of your story and the architect of your behavior. It colors what you see and edits the script in real time, deleting possibilities, rewriting obstacles, cutting scenes of growth before they'll ever have a chance to play out. It decides what gets magnified, what gets minimized, and what gets ignored entirely. It shapes what you believe is possible and what you assume you're worthy of.

And if you don't choose that perspective on purpose, the world will choose it for you.

Same Storm, Different Outcomes

I've worked with dozens of entrepreneurs who have all faced a similar crisis, when external circumstances shift and their business model stops "working." And all of them immediately fall into one of two groups...

The first group asks, "Why is this happening to me? What did I do wrong? How do I get back to where I was?"

The second group asks, "How can I adapt? Where's the opportunity here?"

Same external circumstances. Completely different outcomes. The difference isn't talent or resources. Or even luck. It's the lens they choose to see through.

That's the power of perspective. And it's a choice you have far more control over than you've been choosing.

During the COVID shutdowns, I watched this play out in real time. One client immediately asked, "Where's the opportunity here?" He doubled down on (virtual) client outreach, reorganized his team for remote work, and came out stronger. Another client went silent, froze hiring, and spent months paralyzed by fear. Same external storm. Somewhat similar industries. Same basic resources. But one saw disruption as an opportunity while the other saw it as a disaster. And their chosen lens ultimately determined their outcome.

Those are two of three lenses. The first group is living in one of them. The second group found another. There's a third most people never reach.

Three Perspectives

This isn't about positive thinking. It's about power. And that power starts with choosing one of three perspectives. Because your perspective isn't just descriptive, it's predictive. The lens you choose sets the trajectory for everything that follows. Psychologists have studied this for decades. They call it locus of control, and the people who believe their actions shape their outcomes consistently do better than the people who don't.

There are three fundamental perspectives you can adopt in any given situation.

First, there's the victim perspective. "This is happening to me." This lens makes you a passenger in your own life, as you have chosen to hand over the steering wheel of your vehicle to an external entity. You see yourself as acted upon, not acting. This perspective feels safe to so many because it removes responsibility for outcomes. However, it's the most dangerous perspective you can choose because it also strips away YOUR power.

Power always follows blame.

Second, there's the player perspective. "This is happening, and I can respond." Here, you see yourself as an active participant. You may not have control over all the circumstances, but you can control your responses. This perspective is where most high performers operate. Engaged, responsive, tactical. Not a bad place to be.

But there's a third perspective that creates maximum possibility for your current and future realities, and that's the creator perspective. "This is happening through me" or "This is happening for me." From this lens, you don't just respond to reality. You participate in creating it. Challenges become raw material, each one a chance to transform both the situation and yourself. This is where the extraordinary operate, seeing themselves as authors of their life's story rather than characters in it.

The creator lens doesn't mean everything is easy. Far from it. It means everything is usable. A failed launch becomes data. A betrayal becomes clarity. A setback becomes a forge. You turn pain into rocket fuel. This perspective feels different in your body. Your shoulders drop. Your breathing deepens. Instead of the tight, defensive posture of victim mode or the alert tension of player mode, the creator perspective brings calm intensity. You're authoring your response to whatever unfolds.

I lived all three of these perspectives. When I didn't get the promotion I'd been promised first shot at, the one I'd moved my family across the country for, I spent months in pure victim mode. They lied to me. The system is rigged. Then I shifted into player perspective for about a year and a half. I stopped volunteering extra value, and that was deliberate. I became a competent school leader and chose to leave it there. Tactical. Measured. I played the game with my eyes open, managing my energy like a resource and spending it only where it counted. Not creating anything new yet, but no longer just reacting either. And then, finally, I shifted into creator perspective. *This happened for me.* I'd spent eight years learning how to coach leaders inside an organization. Why not take those skills and build my own practice?

Your perspective shapes more than your responses. It determines what opportunities you can even perceive. The victim perspective makes you blind to possibilities. The player perspective keeps you reactive to circumstances. The creator perspective reveals openings others miss entirely.

And you don't get to choose a creator perspective once and then set and forget it, as if it naturally becomes a "default" mode for you to operate from. You choose it moment by moment, decision by decision. Unfortunately, most of us unconsciously shift into victim mode the moment things become uncomfortable. I've seen this play out thousands of times in coaching sessions. A great leader who operates from a creator's perspective during normal business hours suddenly shifts to a victim mode when he walks in the front door of his home and is confronted by his difficult teenage kids. A parent who empowers their kids to be problem solvers and work from a place of abundance crumbles when trying to individually navigate healthy eating choices when their kids aren't home and no one is watching.

So your perspective is never fixed. Role by role. Pressure by pressure. And that's why awareness is your first line of defense. You can't choose a new perspective until you catch the one you're already in.

See Differently First

You MUST become aware of the automatic perspectives you default to under pressure, and you can start by asking yourself these questions.

When faced with unexpected change, do I automatically interpret it as a threat or an opportunity?

When receiving criticism, do I see it as an attack on my identity or as data points for my growth?

When confronted with challenges or obstacles, do I tell myself... A) This is stopping me, or B) This is teaching me?

These questions might read as simple or even trivial, yet they're anything but. These tiny shifts affect the actions you'll believe as possible and the resources you're willing to tap into, and in turn the results you'll experience. Across all of my client cases, it was rarely the person's capacity for performance that limited them. It was usually their actively chosen perspective. The challenge, though, is that you've most likely never been taught to exercise this choice deliberately. Most people aren't even aware that a choice in perspective is possible. Instead, they've spent years being conditioned to respond automatically rather than intentionally.

But even in the most high-pressure of moments, you always have a split second where active choice is available. The key is recognizing that moment and leveraging it. Start by slowing down your response time. When something triggers you, try to pause instead of immediately reacting. Even a three-second delay can be enough to ask, "How am I choosing to see this right now?" Bring definition to what you're feeling, such as "This feels like a personal attack" or "I'm choosing to see this as a positive." Giving words to our feelings creates space for us to interact with and ultimately influence them. Then try to identify the perspective you're currently operating from: victim, player or creator. Remember, this isn't about judgment. It's about awareness. You can't change what you don't confront.

Then, deliberately choose a more empowering alternative. Find a different angle that's equally true but more useful. Ask yourself, "What's another way I could interpret these same facts that would give me a greater sense of personal agency?"

This takes practice. Tons of practice. But like any skill or mental muscle, conscious perspective choice gets stronger the more you use it.

I use this exercise with almost all of my clients, at some point in their journey. It's messy, but it builds self-trust and pattern awareness fast. You're going to make mistake after mistake as you attempt to improve your choices in perspective. You will react without pausing. You will choose scarcity over abundance. But you will steadily grow and improve as long as you stick with it.

Let's say you get blindsided by a harsh email from a colleague. First instinct? Victim lens... "They're out to get me. This is unfair. Why does this always happen to me?"

Pause. Name it. "I'm seeing this as an attack on my character, and I'm taking it very personal."

Then reframe. "What feedback might be buried in this that could make me better? What if this person is frustrated about something legitimate I can address and learn from?"

That's the pivot. And that's the practice.

The exercise works in four phases.

In the moment. Catch yourself at the point of choice. A few moments can create the space needed to pick your lens instead of defaulting to one.

Right after. How did that go? What worked, what didn't, what did you learn about how you saw it?

End of day. Name 2-3 moments where your perspective shaped your response. What lens were you in? What would a creator's have looked like?

End of week. Review your defaults. Which situations reliably drop you into victim or player mode? Where do you need the most practice?

The Lens Sets the Path

If you lose a major client, you could interpret it as one of three things.

1. A catastrophe (victim perspective)

2. A problem to solve (player perspective)

3. Clarification of who you're meant to serve (creator perspective)

All three could be valid interpretations of the same event. But only one expands your sense of possibility and agency. The perspective you choose will determine the resources you access, the actions you take, and, ultimately, the future you create.

I still have victim reactions, and I coach this for a living. The work is recognizing the lens and recalibrating. Some days, shifting from victim to player is the win. Take it. I do. Nobody lives in the creator lens full-time, including the guy writing this chapter.

The difference now is that I don't unpack my baggage and live in the victim lens anymore. I look around the room, nod my head, and then I get the hell out.

The Truth

Your perspective isn't a personality trait. It's a decision you're making constantly, most of the time without realizing it.

Victim, player, creator. You're always in one of those three. And whichever one you're in is determining what you can even see as possible, not just how you feel about what's in front of you.

You don't get to set your perspective once and forget it. Every pressure point, every hard moment, every walk through the front door after a brutal day. Each is a new choice.

If this one hit hard: Chapter 14 (Beliefs Are the Blueprint) goes deeper on the invisible architecture running your defaults. Chapter 15 (Your Real Values Show Up in Hard Choices) shows you where your real perspective reveals itself when the stakes are highest.

MINI: Stop Being a Side Character in Your Own Life.

Most people are extras in their own movie... And somehow they're proud of it.

They show up every day, hit their (likely below average) marks, deliver their lines ("Yes, boss," "Whatever you think is best," "I'm fine with either"), and go home feeling productive. Meanwhile, the main characters are out there taking risks and actually living interesting lives.

Extras love being extras, even if they won't admit it out loud. It's safe. Predictable. No one expects much from you. You can't really fail if you're not really trying, or get rejected if you never put yourself out there. You can't disappoint anyone if you never promise anything meaningful.

But extras don't get character development. They don't get story arcs. And they definitely don't get the awesome ending.

Sadly, very few people even realize they've been cast into the background of their own story. They think they're the protagonist because they're busy all day. But being busy isn't the same as being important.

You say yes to everyone else's emergencies while your dreams collect dust. You solve other people's problems while avoiding your own. You're incredible at making everyone else's life work better while yours stays exactly the same. And the worst part? You get rewarded for it. You become exceptional at being background scenery... And you start mistaking that for a good life. You're the most competent supporting character anyone could ask for. Need someone reliable? That's you. Need someone who won't rock the boat? Also you. Need someone who'll take on extra work without complaining? Always you.

But competence in the wrong part is still the wrong life.

I'll say it again for everyone in the back...

<u>COMPETENCE IN THE WRONG PART IS STILL THE WRONG LIFE</u>.

I worked with a client (brilliant woman, natural leader) who had been running support for everyone around her for so long that she'd forgotten what it felt like to lead her own life. Her calendar was full of other people's priorities. Her energy was spent solving other people's problems, and her dreams had become something she thought about in the car between errands.

When I asked her what she would do if she treated herself like the main character of her own story, she went silent. Then she meekly replied... "I don't even remember what I want for myself anymore."

If you live in the wrong role long enough, your voice doesn't just get quiet, it disappears. And when it's gone, you lose more than your dreams. You lose your direction. You lose your purpose. You perfect the art of making everyone else's dreams happen while yours fade into "someday."

And the longer you stay a side character, the harder it becomes to remember what your own story was supposed to look like.

Your kids don't need another functional adult in the background. They need someone to model what it looks like to go after what matters. Your colleagues don't need another yes-person, they need someone with actual opinions worth hearing. You don't need to be more helpful, you need to be more alive.

That's the choice in front of you. Keep being indispensable in everyone else's story, or start writing your own.

Main characters make things happen. They don't wait for things to happen to them. They have conversations that extras never get to have. They take risks that background actors avoid. They build things, break and fix things. Because the story doesn't move on its own. They move it.

The story is happening, with or without you. Other people are out there living the life you keep assuring yourself that you'll have "someday." But someday isn't a day of the week. And you weren't put here to be background scenery in someone else's movie.

Write down one decision you've been putting off. You know what to do. You've just been waiting for someone else to validate it or give you permission to move forward.

Then make the decision. Today. The timing won't be perfect. You won't have all the answers. Decide anyway, because extras wait for direction. Main characters give it.

Chapter 3

Promise Debt: Why You Can't Trust Your Own Word.

THE LIE: You've broken promises to yourself before, but that's just part of being human. After all, each one is its own isolated failure. Not a pattern with a compounding cost.
WHY IT HOLDS: Because in your mind, every broken promise comes with a perfectly reasonable explanation. The timing was off. Life got busy, and you'll do better next time. But you don't see that your subconscious is keeping score even when you aren't.

You don't believe yourself anymore. And you shouldn't.

You've created what I call "Promise Debt", the accumulated damage from every commitment you've broken to yourself. Every skipped workout is a withdrawal from your self-trust account. Every "I'll start Monday" that never happens is interest compounding on your credibility deficit.

Two things live inside that account, and most people only ever feel one of them. There's the read you can feel, your gut read on whether your own word is good for anything. Call that self-trust. Before you ever attempt a single thing today, it's the voice that tells you whether you'll actually follow through this time. Underneath it sits the record, the running ledger of what you've actually done when it counted. That's self-reputation. Self-trust is what you feel. Self-reputation is what's true. Keep them separate, because you can't "believe your way" into the feeling without also doing the work that builds the record. Affirmations can nudge the feeling for an afternoon. But it's a temporary high, and it's why you keep running back to motivation porn. Only kept promises rebuild your account balance. And the feeling (self-trust) always snaps back to match the balance (self-reputation), because your subconscious only cares about the account balance. Not pep talks.

Just like financial debt, Promise Debt has been building quietly in the background. And the bank you can't get credit from anymore? That's you.

The Bankruptcy You Can't See

Just like financial debt compounds with interest, Promise Debt accumulates faster than you realize. You make small compromises here and there. Negotiate with your own standards, then delay tough decisions. And each broken promise compounds the damage.

The breakdown follows a predictable pattern.

- **Small Defaults:** "I'll wake up at 6AM" becomes 6:30, then 7:00, then whenever...
- **Negotiated Standards:** "I'll work out 4 times a week" becomes "Well, 3 is still good. Maybe two..." Or none.
- **Delayed Decisions:** "I'll have that difficult conversation soon" becomes a never-ending cycle of kicking that can down the road.
- **Conditional Commitments:** "I'll start when I feel ready" (spoiler: you'll never "feel" ready) becomes waiting forever for those perfect circumstances to appear.

How do these look in action? Or in other words, how do you drain your self-reputation balances on a daily basis?

- "I'll stop checking my phone first thing in the morning." Broken before you're even fully awake. You grab your phone to turn the alarm off and Instagram is open before your eyes even are.
- "I'll eat clean starting tomorrow." Said for the 27th consecutive day. And some days you even start strong, until the sugar cravings get you in the evenings. And you know this!
- "I'll meditate for just 5 minutes daily." You even put it on your calendar. You even get a session going some days... But then abandon it the moment you feel comfortable.

Every broken promise does more than fail to create change. It actively undermines your belief that change is even possible. Your subconscious learns not to trust anything you say about your own future.

This is the behavior loop, working against you. If behavior is the key to influencing your beliefs, then Promise Debt is the machine running negative proof. Every broken promise is evidence for the internal narrative that already suspects you won't follow through. Same loop, same currency... Just spent against the person you're trying to build.

Think of your self-reputation like a credit score. Break enough promises, and you're in identity foreclosure. Your word carries no weight, not even to yourself. Miss a morning routine? That's $100 in trust debt. Say "I'll start Monday" and don't? Overdraft fee. Negotiate with your own standards? That's another late payment.

Eventually, the Bank of Self-Reputation closes. You've defaulted too many times.

The good news? Just like financial debt and your real-life credit score, your self-reputation can be rebuilt. But it requires treating your word like the valuable currency it is. Especially the promises no one else will ever know about.

The Path of Recovery

If you're reading this and thinking "I'm already too far gone", let me stop you right there.

I built this framework because I lived it. During my zombie years (the two and a half years after the promotion that never came) I had a Sunday ritual where I would map out "my best week". Up everyday by 5AM and hitting the gym before work. Home in time for dinner, and try to get there early enough for me to be the cook. Real time with my girls, no phone. No video games. It felt like intention, definitely looked like a great plan. But by Monday afternoon it was already in rubble. By Tuesday I'd given up completely and slipped back into reactive mode. And the next Sunday would come again and I'd do the exact same thing... Plan a week that would never happen. For over two years the debt didn't just pile up in my habits, it piled up in my identity. I had completely stopped being someone who showed up for his own self. That's not a coaching observation. That's a confession.

But the depth of your Promise Debt doesn't disqualify you from recovery. Hell, it makes your recovery even more valuable when you've pulled it off, especially to the person that matters most. YOU.

I've worked with people who hadn't kept a single commitment to themselves in years. People who couldn't stick to a morning routine for three days. People who had given up on themselves so completely that the idea of setting another goal felt like some sick joke.

The mistake they all made initially was trying to climb out of Promise Debt the same way they fell into it... With big, dramatic commitments. "I'm going to transform my entire life starting Monday." "I'm going to work out every day, eat perfectly, wake up at 5AM, and meditate for an hour."

But that's not recovery. That's Promise Debt on steroids. It's the guy at the casino that keeps doubling every losing bet because "he has to hit it big at some point" and instead loses everything he owns. Real recovery starts with what I call impossible-to-fail commitments. These are about becoming undeniable. The goal is to prove to your subconscious that you can trust yourself with something, anything, again. You're not trying to change your life on day one.

When you're in Promise Debt bankruptcy, your subconscious is like a jaded investor. It wants to see small, consistent returns before it'll trust you with bigger investments. So you start embarrassingly small. Drink one glass of water when you wake up. Make your bed. Write one sentence in a journal. Walk to the mailbox. Do one single push-up. These aren't life-changing habits, they're trust-building exercises. Which is exactly what you need.

You'll resist this approach because it feels like settling for the small and mundane. It's not. It's strategic recovery. You're trying to become someone who keeps their word. First to themselves, then to the world. And that identity shift happens one micro-promise at a time.

The beautiful thing about starting from Promise Debt bankruptcy is that every small win carries more weight. When you've disappointed yourself 1000 times, keeping one tiny promise for seven days in a row feels like a miracle. Because it is.

You're not just building habits. You're rebuilding your relationship with your own word. You're rebuilding your self-reputation. And that relationship is the foundation everything else in your life is built on.

The Confidence Trap

Some of the most chronically stuck people I've coached *looked* nothing like stuck. Confident in rooms and charismatic under pressure. The kind of presence that makes everyone else sit up a little straighter. But ask them to sit alone for an hour without their phone, and they'd start unraveling. Ask them to say no to a social situation they knew wasn't aligned with their core values, and they'd fold. If I pushed them to keep a commitment when no one was watching... They'd quickly find a reason to avoid our next couple of conversations.

The confidence everyone else saw in them wasn't real evidence of a strong self-reputation. It was energy management. A performance polished over years of practice.

And we've built an entire culture around this. Belief gets handed out before it's been earned. By influencers, by well-meaning parents, by a self-help industry that sells you the feeling of momentum as a substitute for the thing itself. **The result is a generation fluent in the language of growth and illiterate in the practice of it.** They can tell you exactly what discipline looks like, they just can't show you.

Confidence built on performance instead of proof isn't actually confidence. It's a front. And that front holds up fine... At least until the pressure gets real.

The Evidence Equation

When it comes to self-trust, almost everyone assumes it's something you generate from within. It's not. It's something you witness.

You don't need to believe you're capable. You need to see yourself being capable.

You don't need affirmations about your strength. You need evidence of your strength.

Real self-trust comes from a simple equation.

Evidence + Repetition = Earned Trust

When you say you'll do something and then do it (especially when it's hard, especially when no one's watching, especially when you don't feel like it) you make a deposit in your self-trust account.

Let me show you what this looks like in practice.

Day 1: You set your alarm for 6AM. You wake up at 6AM. You hate it. Your body wants five more minutes, but you get up anyway. That's one piece of evidence that you can trust your word.

Day 3: You promised yourself you'd have that difficult conversation with your teammate. Every instinct screams to postpone it, but you have the conversation anyway. That's evidence you can handle discomfort.

Day 7: You committed to writing for 20 minutes daily. Today, you have zero inspiration. You end up writing garbage for 20 minutes that you know you'll end up deleting. That's evidence you show up regardless of how you feel.

Over time, these micro-wins start stacking. Individually they're not impressive. But together they're building something more valuable than any single achievement. They're building your identity as someone who keeps their word. And after 30 days of micro-evidence, trusting yourself becomes your default mode. Your track record makes doubt unreasonable.

The counterexample? The person who says "I'll start next week" but always finds a reason why this week wasn't the right time. They're collecting evidence too. Evidence that their word means nothing, that change is always conditional and they can't be trusted to follow through.

Self-trust doesn't start with swagger. It snowballs from a quiet commitment to the intentionally mundane.

The Private Transformation

I worked with a sales director who looked like huge success from every external angle. Custom cars, big house, respect from his peers. Wall-to-wall awards very visible in his office.

And right next to these awards? Framed quotes about excellence and persistence. He had subscriptions to every business newsletter, read all the leadership books. He listened to all the right podcasts during his commutes and even his workouts. He could recite Tony Robbins, Simon Sinek, and every other expert you can think of.

But he couldn't look himself in the mirror without getting super twitchy and uncomfortable.

Professionally, he was thriving. Privately, he was failing. And he was avoiding that reality through more hits of motivation porn.

Every morning, he'd set his alarm for 5AM to work out before the family woke up. And every morning he'd hit snooze until there was no time left. He'd promise his wife he'd be home for dinner, then get "trapped" in meetings that could have easily ended an hour earlier. He'd commit to weekly one-on-ones with his team, then consistently reschedule when "bigger opportunities" appeared. He'd promise his son he'd make his soccer game on Saturday. Then miss it again for another "work crisis."

Small breaks. Tiny compromises. Nothing that would show up on his performance review, but everything that was destroying his ability to ever trust his own word again.

The breaking point came on a Tuesday evening. He was sitting in his car outside his house, engine off and incapable of any kind of focus. His wife had texted asking when he'd be home for dinner. Again. His son had a game that weekend he'd probably miss. Again. And he'd promised himself he'd start working out "next week" for the past eight months.

In that moment, fidgeting, he scrolled past his own earlier LinkedIn post about "authentic leadership"... And he felt physically sick. The content from the post wasn't wrong. He just knew he was living none of it. The gap between his public persona and private reality had become a chasm he could no longer ignore.

That's when he realized he wasn't just failing to live up to his own standards. He had stopped believing he ever would again. The kicker? All that motivational content was making it worse. Every quote on his wall felt like a lie. Every podcast about discipline reminded him of his own lack of it. Every book about leadership highlighted the gap between who he appeared to be and who he actually was.

He had become fluent in the language of success without living it in his own life. He could parrot the right words about integrity and discipline, but those words felt hollow because his private actions weren't aligned with their message.

He avoided his family because he felt like a fraud. He dodged team meetings because he didn't feel prepared. He ran from situations where he might hear "no"... And this from a guy in sales leadership.

His resume was elite. His self-reputation was broken.

The motivational quotes weren't inspiring him, they were condemning him. Because deep down, he knew he wasn't living up to the wisdom he was consuming. He had all the right answers but none of the right actions.

That's the danger of trying to think your way into confidence. Knowledge without action can quickly spiral into another form of self-deception.

The Micro-Promise Solution

We kept it small and we started with two questions. What does a good day look like? What is he currently avoiding? We spent a week building a daily practice of answering these questions. Then we took that momentum and built an incredibly simple protocol. Every morning, he would define what a good day looks like (work goals, family needs). Include some micro-promises to himself, never more than three in total. If he's avoiding something he has to set time to attack it. And every night he would take 15 minutes to measure how he lived up to that.

The key was small promises made daily to himself. Especially in the places he used to run from.

The tough phone call goes on the calendar. Family time becomes mandatory, and also on the calendar. Skipped workouts? You can't sleep until you sweat for at least 15 minutes. Hard conversations? Scheduled, not avoided.

As he started keeping those promises to himself, the quotes on his walls started feeling LIVED instead of aspirational. The books began feeling like validation of his efforts instead of condemnation for their (past) lack.

And his performance across his life leveled up in ways that surprised everyone around him, especially himself. He hadn't found a new system or a growth hack. He'd stopped trying to outrun the gap between how he looked and who he was. He had finally started living up to all those quotes he'd been staring at and parroting for years.

Your Mirror Moment

Stop for a second and put down the productivity techniques and transformation strategies.

What's one area of your life where your self-reputation is really suffering? An area of your life where the Promise Debt has grown to uncomfortable levels? Where you instinctively flinch before making a new promise because you already know you'll break it?

Maybe it's fitness. Maybe it's that side project you keep "meaning to start." Maybe it's the boundaries you keep saying you'll set but never enforce. Maybe it's the simple daily habits that could set off a cascade of dominoes across your life (meditating, journaling, spending more time with your kids) if you could just stick to them.

That area, the one that made you uncomfortable just thinking about it, that's where your transformation begins. With one painfully small, painfully honest micro-win.

What you're building through micro-promises isn't a to-do list. It's your self-reputation. And it's the most valuable asset you'll ever own.

CHALLENGE

For the next seven days, practice micro-promises. These are commitments so small that breaking them would be embarrassing.

1. Choose ONE tiny daily commitment (drink water when you wake up, make your bed, write three sentences).
2. Do it for seven consecutive days.
3. Track your completion rate.
4. Notice how keeping/breaking these micro-promises affects your inner dialogue.

And if you miss a day? Don't spiral. Log it as data. Ask why, reassess and redesign. Then recommit. Your relationship with your word is also built through the repairs, not just the reps.

The goal is rebuilding your relationship with your own word. Start small. Start private. And start today.

The Truth

You don't have a motivation problem. You have a self-reputation problem. Built one broken promise at a time, quietly, over years.

The bank you can't get credit from anymore is you. And no amount of inspiration or productivity systems fixes that. Only kept promises do. Small ones. Private ones. The ones nobody else will ever know about.

Your self-reputation isn't a concept. It's the foundation everything else is sitting on.

If this one hit hard: Chapter 12 (This Is Where You Always Quit) is where rebuilding self-reputation through action becomes the actual construction method. Chapter 18 (The Work Evolves. It Never Ends.) deals with what it looks like to keep showing up after the early momentum fades, which is exactly where Promise Debt comes back for most people.

Chapter 4

Take the Damn Wheel.

THE LIE: You're not where you want to be, and you didn't put yourself here. The timing, the economy, the people who let you down... They built your situation. And what you didn't break isn't yours to fix.
WHY IT HOLDS: Because the reasons are real. The obstacles happened, they cost you something, and naming them feels like honesty. So you stop there, at the true part. But "not my fault" and "not my responsibility" aren't the same thing.

You're on your couch, scrolling through social media, watching other people live the life you claim you want. Your resume hasn't been updated in months. Your gym membership is collecting dust.

Essentially, your dreams are on permanent pause.

But you've got a hell of a story ready for anyone who asks how things are going. "The market is tough right now." "My boss doesn't appreciate me." "If the right opportunity would just come along, I'm ready for it."

Stop. Seriously, just fucking stop.

You can rebuild self-reputation all day through micro-promises. And you should. But if you're still waiting for someone else to change your life, you've just built a nicer cage. Self-trust gives you the potential needed to get in motion. Ownership is what takes the first step.

Remember when I told you I used to drown in inspiration but live unchanged? That was the cost of waiting for a plan, for a breakthrough to be handed to me. Something to come along and "save me." That hoped-for something came in the form of online courses, podcasts, books, and social media accounts. None of these are wrong on their own, but it's the expectations you bring to them that can prove damaging.

But once you rebuild trust in yourself, blame becomes the real enemy. And blame is just disguised helplessness. I'll share two truths that will either wake you up or piss you off. I'll take either, so long as you're willing to look in the mirror and get very real with yourself.

Truth #1: No one is coming to save you. Not your boss, not your partner, not the government, not the universe. The cavalry isn't coming because YOU are the cavalry.

Truth #2: Where you place blame determines where your power goes. Every finger you point outward is power you're handing away.

They're the most liberating truths you'll ever face. But only if you're brave enough to stop running from them. Back in Chapter 2, the victim's first move was handing over the wheel. This is where you take it back.

The Victim's Waiting Room

Most people are sitting in a waiting room. And they've been there so long that they've forgotten they could leave. Waiting for the right opportunity to knock. Waiting for someone to recognize their potential, or for their circumstances to improve. Waiting for courage to finally show up and push you to take action.

And while they wait, they blame.

They blame their childhood for their fears. They blame their spouse for their unhappiness. They blame the economy for their financial struggles. They blame their genetics for their health problems. They blame society for not giving them a fair shot.

Every minute spent blaming is hours forfeited from building. And with each external attribution, you willingly give away another piece of your power. You become a permanent patient in this waiting room... Stuck. Complaining. But never leaving. That's how waiting and blaming work together to destroy your future. They're different distractions in the same waiting room. One's the magazine you flip through mindlessly, the other's the TV droning in the background. Both keep you occupied and feeling like you're doing something, and both ensure you never get up and leave.

When you blame external factors for the conditions of your life, you're not just avoiding responsibility. You're actively choosing powerlessness. Blame feels good in the moment. It protects your ego. It makes you feel righteous. But there's a cost so massive it will steal your entire future if you let it. **Every time you point the finger at someone else, you're saying, "My future depends on them changing, not me."**

Read that again. It's that fucking important because that's exactly what you're doing, to yourself and your future.

This power transfer happens whether your blame is justified or not. You might be 100% right about who wronged you. Your complaints might be completely valid. The system might actually be rigged against you. But being right about who's to blame won't build you a better life.

Only taking ownership of what happens next can do that.

You're Right... So What Now?

Many people will choose to close this book in this moment and go back to their comfortable victim story. But if you're still reading, it means some part of you knows I'm right.

Yes, it's not your fault the economy crashed and you lost your job. But what skills did you develop during the good times? How much did you save? What's your plan now, networking or complaining?

Yes, it's not your fault your partner cheated and destroyed your marriage. But what red flags did you ignore? How long did you avoid the hard conversations and play your own role in pushing them away? What patterns will you break before your next relationship?

Yes, it's not your fault you grew up with dysfunction and trauma. But are you getting help? Are you breaking generational cycles? Are you going to pass your damage onto your kids, or heal it?

I know you want a better life. So how's blaming the world working out for you so far?

Look, you're not responsible for what happened to you. But you are responsible for what you do about it. That's the difference between victim and victor. Victims stay married to the story of what was done to them. Victors divorce that story and write a new chapter based on what they'll do about it.

When Isaac's parents hired me to work with their 26-year-old son, he was a walking blame machine. Failed out of college? The professors were unfair and his high school didn't prepare him. Couldn't get a job? The economy was rigged and employers were discriminatory. Living in his parents' basement while playing video games 14 hours a day? Society had failed his generation, not his fault.

Isaac had an explanation for everything, and not a single one of them involved Isaac.

After he blew through two retail jobs in three weeks, both times walking out when managers addressed his tardiness and attitude, I sat him down for what would become our breakthrough session.

"Isaac, help me understand something. You've now lost two jobs in three weeks. Two different managers, two totally different places. What do you think is going on here?"

Silence.

"I mean, what are the odds that both managers just happened to be complete jerks who immediately had it out for you?"

He shifted in his chair. Started rattling off reasons why both jobs were unfair, how neither manager understood his situation, how the expectations were unrealistic.

I let him talk. Then I asked the question that (I hoped) would cut through all of the noise between us...

"Okay, but who's the common denominator in both situations?"

The Breaking Point

We did a detective session where we break down every failure and every excuse, piece by piece. Who chose not to set an alarm? Who decided that being late wasn't a big deal? Who quit instead of having a difficult conversation? Who made the choice to prioritize video games over job preparation?

Each answer stripped away another layer of his victim armor. After 45 minutes, Isaac slumped back and said, "Okay, fine. Maybe I could have handled some things differently."

That was the crack in the wall. And once Isaac stopped asking "Why is this happening to me?" and started asking "What am I going to do about it?" his whole frame moved. Not overnight, since it took months to fully take effect. But he didn't quit and pushed through the resistance.

Within the year, Isaac had landed an entry-level coding job and moved into his own apartment. But what struck me was his mindset.

"You know what's crazy?" he said. "I used to think everyone was just out to screw me over. Like my professors, my old managers, whatever. And maybe some of that stuff was unfair, I don't know. But sitting around being pissed about it wasn't helping me at all. Once I stopped waiting for other people to fix my problems and just started handling my own shit, things got easier."

And taking ownership did more than just change Isaac internally. He discovered it attracted the help he'd been waiting for. His coding bootcamp instructors started investing extra time in him. Potential employers reached out to him when he followed up on his applications with calls and emails. "It's weird," Isaac told me months later. "When I was blaming everyone, nobody wanted to help me. Now that I own my stuff, it feels like people want to see me succeed." **Nobody invests in victims. But everyone wants to support someone who's working to improve.**

The Choice

The realization that will either change your life or make you hate this book? Every day you spend waiting for someone to save you is making your situation actively worse.

Momentum takes work. Decay is automatic. Every day you stay stuck, your bad habits become more entrenched, your excuses become more comfortable and your self-trust becomes weaker. One day of blame doesn't equal one day of building. The hole gets deeper. The climb gets steeper.

You think you're protecting yourself. After all, you're just being realistic. You're not, though. You're just scared. Scared that if you stop blaming, you'll have to face how much of your life is your fault. Scared that if you stop waiting for rescue, you'll have to do the hard work yourself.

And I get it. You might even be thinking, "But what about genuine injustice? What about trauma? What about things that really aren't my fault?"

You're right. Life isn't fair. Some people get dealt a shitty hand, and some carry wounds they didn't ask for. But do you want sympathy, or do you want freedom?

Because whether you want understanding from others or freedom from your circumstances, the work in front of you is the same.

You can acknowledge that life is unfair AND still refuse to make that your excuse. You can grieve over what was done to you AND still take responsibility for what you do about it. You can hate your shitty circumstances AND still own every choice you make in response.

Is your blame making you stronger? Is it really building your future? Or are you just bleeding out your future to protect a wound from your past?

If you're ready to stop being a passenger in your own life, this is how you start...

Replace "Why is this happening to me?" with "What am I going to do about it?"

Stop waiting for perfect conditions. Start where you are, with what you have, right now. Own your choices, all of them. They're all yours. And they all led you here.

Ask better questions. Instead of "Who can I blame?" ask "What can I control?"

And we can put all of this into practice.

Track Your Language: Start catching yourself in real time. "They never told me" becomes "I didn't ask." "It's impossible in this economy" becomes "I need a different strategy." "My boss doesn't appreciate me" becomes "I need to create even more value or find somewhere that will recognize my worth."

The 24-Hour Ownership Experiment: For one full day, ban all external explanations. Every frustration, setback, or problem gets the same response, "What's my part in this, and what can I do about it?" It's harder than it sounds and more revealing than you'd expect.

Handle the Resistance: Your brain will fight this. It'll serve up perfectly valid reasons why your situation really is different. Why that person really WAS wrong or why the system really IS rigged. Don't argue with these thoughts and instead just ask, "And now what?" Even if your brain is 100% right, blame still doesn't build your future.

Micro-Ownership Moments: Ownership lives in small choices, and these are powerful leverage points to break these internal victim cycles. Taking the stairs instead of complaining about being out of shape, or making the call instead of waiting for them to reach out first. Admitting "I don't know" rather than pretending you do. These moments teach your brain that you're someone who acts, not someone who just complains.

The moment you shift from external blame to internal responsibility, you stop being a side character in your story and finally step into the leading part. Victims will never be the lead.

You don't have to like it. You don't have to think it's fair. You just have to choose ownership. The power was always yours. You just gave it away.

And ownership might not be the end of the journey, but it's at least the beginning of a life that's yours again.

CONFESSION

Write this sentence: "I've been waiting for _______ to change before I take action."

Fill in the blank. Your boss. Your partner. The economy. Your circumstances. Your motivation level.

Say it out loud. That's your false savior.

Now write the next line: "No one is coming. I have to _______."

Fill in that blank, too. That's your rescue mission.

You've been waiting forever for someone to come and save you. But that person was you. It always was. And the time is now.

The Truth

Blame feels like clarity. It's not. It's just a story that keeps you in the waiting room while your future compounds in the wrong direction.

You're not responsible for everything that happened to you, but you are responsible for everything that happens next. And that's the only distinction that matters.

The power was always yours. You just kept handing it away.

If this one hit hard: Chapter 15 (Your Real Values Show Up in Hard Choices) shows you where ownership actually lives, not in intention but in what you choose when something real is on the line. Chapter 16 (You Can't Win the Game If You're Playing the Wrong Role) is about showing up as the right version of yourself in the moments that matter most.

Chapter 5

You Can't Skip the Desert.

THE LIE: If the process is working, you should be able to feel it working. Progress is visible. Momentum is noticeable. If nothing seems to be happening then something is probably wrong, and you should quit this effort.
WHY IT HOLDS: Because it's how every transformation story gets told after the fact. Nobody films the Desert. So when you're inside it, the silence feels like proof you're failing instead of proof you're in the middle.

You've taken ownership. You've stopped waiting for rescue. You're done making excuses.

So now what?

This is where a lot of people, having finally grabbed the wheel, drive straight into a ditch. Ownership gets you behind the wheel. A process is what keeps you on the road.

You've seen this pattern before. You get fired up, take massive action for two weeks, then burn out when nothing seems to be working. You blame the goal, the timing, or even yourself. But the real problem was that you tried to sprint a marathon. Ownership gives you permission to move, and that's foundational work. But sustainable transformation also requires understanding the actual process of becoming someone new, in a way that sticks when life gets hard.

That's where the Identity Engine comes in.

You're probably asking by now, "How do I actually make this change stick?"

The answer, though, isn't what most people want to hear because they're still staring at the wrong scoreboard. They're measuring the gap instead of the gain, obsessing over the outcome and ignoring the process. They stare at the mountaintop and never take the step right in front of them.

But real change doesn't happen in the result. It happens in the becoming, through what I call the Identity Engine. The process that builds the kind of person who can hold the outcomes you're hungering for.

The Identity Engine

Outcomes don't create identity. I get it, that's jarring to read. But believing that they do has cost you years of progress.

Identity creates outcomes.

Most people try to achieve first, then become. The thought is they'll find success and then internally adapt to this new state of being. They want the promotion, then they'll become a great leader. If they just get married, then they'll be a partner who knows how to love and is worthy of love. But this backwards approach is why so many stay stuck. They're waiting for external permission to become who they need to be. They think the title will make them confident, or the money will make them generous.

But your external world responds to your identity NOW.

The Identity Engine embraces this truth. **Become first, achieve second.** Behave like the person who already has what you want. Do this consistently and the external results become inevitable. But becoming that person happens through a process. And every real process involving identity change has three phases that you can't skip, hack, or shortcut. Understanding them can help you stay the course when others would bail. Because the giving up almost always happens in Phase 2, the Desert. They can't handle the silence, the doubt, the seeming lack of progress. They retreat to motivation porn and they keep searching for new strategies or the next trendy growth hack.

But in doing so you miss something crucial. The Desert is where champions are forged. It's where you learn to move without external validation. Where you develop the antifragility that separates those who succeed once from those who succeed consistently.

Underneath the phases is the behavior loop, and it plays a staggering role in determining whether you make it through all three phases. It's running under every action you take, either feeding the identity you're building or reinforcing the old story that kept you small. The snooze button. The phone grab. The email you answer while the work you promised sits there. Thousands of reps a day, each one handing the belief layer another piece of evidence about who you are. Left unsupervised, those reps have been manufacturing proof of the old self for years. And you can't referee thousands of choices with willpower. Nobody can. So you build the Engine. You take the damn wheel and design the defaults, and the reps start reinforcing the new identity. And the internal debate decreases over time. The phases below are what that takeover feels like from the inside... From the first deliberate reps, through the long stretch where the count climbs and nothing seems to move, to the day the volume tips and the Engine starts running itself.

Phase 1: The Enthusiasm Gap

This is where your journey begins, full of fire and driven by vision. You can see the summit and it feels attainable. You're building momentum. The work feels fresh, exciting, aligned with your values.

But enthusiasm has a very short half-life. And without structure, it breaks down into guilt and shame. Most people quit when their enthusiasm fades. They mistake feeling good for being committed. They think motivation should sustain them. But motivation is often like junk food for your psychology. It gives you a quick bump of energy, then leaves you feeling emptier than before. And it almost never survives sustained confrontation with resistance (both internal and external) and with the first signs that this might be harder than you anticipated.

This is why New Year's resolutions fail by February. Why gym memberships go unused after March, and why business plans collect dust after the initial excitement of creating them wears off. **People try to build their transformations on the shakiest possible foundation... How they feel.**

But the people who do make it through Phase 1, though, learn something crucial. Enthusiasm gets you started, but systems keep you moving forward.

Phase 2: The Desert

This is where the real separation happens between those who build a new identity and those who just liked the idea of one. The excitement is gone and results are nowhere in sight. The journey feels longer than you expected. Way longer.

This is the Desert. No cheering crowds. No quick validation. Just you and the promises made to yourself about the person you're committed to becoming.

This is where you build character. Where you learn to move without external motivation or affirmation. Where you prove your promises to yourself weren't just words, and you stop relying on how you feel and start relying on who you are.

The Desert teaches you the most valuable skill in human performance, which is the ability to act regardless of your internal state. You learn to show up when you don't want to or don't feel like it. To keep promises to yourself when nobody else is watching, and to trust the process when the evidence isn't there yet.

I know what that place feels like. When I left education and started building my coaching practice, I had a network that could have funded my first two years if I'd just committed to picking up the phone... But I didn't. I have social anxiety. Networking events feel like a slow suffocation and small talk feels like a trap. So instead of doing the thing that would actually work, I did the things that *felt* like work. Another online course promising a paint-by-numbers coaching practice of my dreams. Another marketing system promising to fill my pipeline with new prospects. Same drug, different dealer. And I freaking knew better. I was literally building a business to help people recognize (and avoid) that exact pattern. The hardest part to recognize was that I was never lazy. I worked my ass off, but being busy doesn't mean I was being effective. I had to accept the Desert was punishing me for being a hypocrite.

Most quit here. They can't handle the silence and the internal doubt. They assume the process is broken because any signs of visible progress feel like they've dried up. But those who can make it to the other side of the Desert? They enter the final phase, where the extraordinary life is formed.

Phase 3: Momentum

After enough consistent action, the work begins to feel natural and results start to compound. What was once difficult becomes your new normal.

You've built evidence-based momentum. Now the process starts to pull you, rather than you pushing the process. And this is where the Identity Engine proves itself. Where the transformation becomes visible to everyone, including you. Where you start to express your identity rather than just execute the process. Where people start asking what you're doing differently, not realizing you've been doing it for months in the Desert.

But there are no shortcuts to Phase 3. There is no magic hack through the transformation. You can't skip the Desert. You can't outsource the becoming.

Why Process Beats Outcome Every Time

When you focus on outcomes, you're always measuring yourself against what you don't have yet. That gap feels like failure and it creates anxiety, impatience, and the constant temptation to change strategies. But when you focus on process (and in turn, progress) you're measuring yourself against your own previous performance. That's where evidence accumulates and identity shifts from aspiration to reality. And that's where confidence lives.

Process builds what outcome-chasing can't touch.

Self-reputation. When you make a promise to yourself and keep it (especially when it's hard), you build a reservoir of confidence that no external validation can match. Every time you show up when you don't want to, you prove to yourself that you can be counted on. This becomes the foundation for all other aspects of your personal growth. This is Promise Debt in action.

Pattern recognition. When you do the work consistently, you start to see patterns. Where is resistance strongest? Which environments support your growth? What time of day yields your best output? What triggers your old habits, and what triggers the new ones you're pursuing? This intelligence is invaluable. But this pattern recognition can only be constructed through hundreds of repetitions, so you can't shortcut this data collection. You can't get it from a book or a course. You have to earn it through consistent action across different circumstances, energy levels, and life situations. You have to learn it through your own personal grind of planning, acting, and reflecting, over and over again.

Adaptability. Real processes aren't rigid. They evolve as you evolve. You learn to adjust, to refine, and to troubleshoot when needed. When outcome-focused people hit obstacles, they quit. When process-focused people hit obstacles, they adapt. They see problems as information, not judgments.

Antifragility. You don't just withstand stress, you get stronger from it. Process-focused people become antifragile because they've built muscles from resistance. They've learned that discomfort is data and that struggle is growth. And this antifragility is built upon the foundation of an earned confidence that can only come from following through regardless of your circumstances. Never because of them.

Measure the Gain, Not the Gap

If you want to make it through the process, stop fixating on how far you have to go. Instead, start measuring how far you've come.

If you want a better body, then don't measure yourself against the fitness influencer. Measure yourself against your own yesterday. Did you eat with intention? Did you move your body? That's gain.

If you want to grow your business, then don't obsess over someone else's seven-figure launch. Measure the gain from where you started... The pitch you made and the calls you booked.

If you want a stronger relationship with your partner, then don't compare your marriage to what you see on social media. Measure the tough conversation you had (and would have much rather avoided), the shared values you've created together, and the vulnerability you've dared to show.

Progress doesn't live in the future. It lives in your daily execution. But you have to actually track the gain. You think you're measuring your progress, but you're not. You're just feeling your progress. And feelings fluctuate. They lie. They're influenced by your mood and your energy, your sleep, your last meal. Put real numbers to your progress. Vague effort might feel good, but measured progress builds self-reputation.

Track the gains that matter.

- How many days did you really show up this week?
- How many meaningful conversations did you have?
- How much longer can you sustain focused work now versus when you started?
- How many times did you choose the harder "right" over the easier "wrong?"
- How many promises did you keep to yourself?

Let's say you want to become a calm, present parent. You measure that by noticing how many times you paused before reacting and the nights you put the phone down and made eye contact. How are you doing in those areas compared to last week? That's the gain.

Make the invisible visible. Make the progress undeniable.

The Plateau Is Not a Problem

There's a second metaphor I use in my practice, one that captures a more specific version of the Desert experience, and it might be the most disorienting one. The Desert describes the absence of feedback entirely. No signal, no landmarks, nothing. But the plateau is a different paradigm. It's what Phase 2 looks like every time it comes back around. You think you're finally breaking through into Momentum and you've left the Desert behind... Nope. Here, your systems are running. You're showing up and the work is getting done. You even had what felt like a huge breakthrough a couple of months ago. You had a burst of new accounts (if you're in sales). Or you had a week where your marriage felt effortless for the first time in forever. But, once again, the scoreboard has gone completely silent. Most people who are surviving the Desert get ambushed by the plateau because of that burst of results, as it gives them the false feeling they've made it through to the other side. It's an illusion though, and then you settle back into the journey... And the results just won't come consistently enough to keep you encouraged. It feels like the classic two steps forward, three steps back experience. And that gap between consistent effort and visible output is where the mastery curve gets misread as a malfunction.

I ask people all the time to chart what they believe a line representing personal transformation looks like, and they respond with an almost perfectly straight line that's sloping upwards. But this is horribly wrong, and that misconception breaks people when their growth encounters the plateau. I then explain to them that the line should look like the steps of a stairway, but with the flat portions extending much further than the periodic vertical lines of breakthrough growth.

The plateau is where your commitment gets tested without the reward of consistent, visible progress. Where you learn to move forward on faith in yourself and your process, rather than results. Where the deep, invisible growth happens... Your capacity expanding. Your foundation strengthening.

And the thing is, you won't *feel* any of it. The plateau actually feels like stagnation. Like you're spinning your wheels and you're wasting your time.

Then, suddenly, another huge breakthrough occurs. After enough consistent action through the plateau (through that step of the stairway), something breaks.

Progress becomes visible again. Often exponentially so. What seemed like weeks or months of "no movement" was instead the quiet buildup to a quantum leap. But you only get the breakthrough if you honor the plateau.

This is where the process (the Desert and plateau) teaches you its most valuable lesson... You don't need external validation to keep moving. You just need loyalty to the person you've promised to become.

Even after I stopped chasing shiny baubles and built real systems (CRM loaded, network mapped, enough consistent outreach to keep referrals moving) I'd still hit two or three months with nothing. Total silence, zero new referrals. And every time, the temptation was to scrap it and start over. I didn't. I would re-audit what had already worked, double down there, and just keep going. Because the plateau is a sign the compound interest hasn't posted yet, and you have to keep investing and just remember the problem isn't in the process.

Design Your Identity Engine

You can't borrow someone else's process and expect it to transform you, no matter how many thousands of online experts will attempt to convince you otherwise. Their process was built for their context, their self-perceptions, their demands, and their psychology. You just won't read that in their sales copy, only that if you just do what they do you'll find the exact same results. It's bullshit.

You MUST design your own Identity Engine.

And this begins with answering the questions most people skip or avoid entirely.

Who must I become to achieve this goal? What skills will you need to acquire? What character traits must you embody? Habits and routines? How does that person make tough decisions?

If you want the six-figure business, you can't just copy tactics. You have to become the kind of person who thinks strategically, makes what feels like impossible decisions based on incomplete information, always follows through consistently, and can hear "no" a hundred times without quitting.

If you want the relationship you've never had, you'll have to do more than learn communication techniques. You have to become someone who sets necessary boundaries, and can love deeply without losing your unique and independent sense of self.

What does daily progress look like? The key word is daily, as in commitment to a daily reflection on the following questions. What must you do today, even if it means not going to bed until it's done? What are the daily promises critical for you to rebuild your self-reputation?

How will I measure the gain? What specific behaviors will prove you're doing the work, even when results aren't visible yet? How can you measure yourself against who you were last week?

What sacrifices am I willing to endure? Anything worth having carries a price. That's the law of opportunity costs, and it's always present. What are you willing to restructure your life around? What will you sacrifice and what pain can you commit to enduring?

What will I do when the plateau hits? Because it will. How will you keep moving forward when progress goes quiet? What will you say to yourself to keep your shoulders squared in the direction you must keep traveling in?

This is an exercise in designing. You're building the framework that will carry you through every phase of transformation. I see this constantly with clients. They skip this step and jump straight into tactics without building the foundation. They start meal prepping before they've become someone who actually values how they eat, or they start networking without becoming someone worthy of meaningful connections. They start posting content without first becoming someone with something meaningful to say, and they get lost in likes and impressions.

The architecture comes first. Not months of research, that's its own trap. Map the identity gap you need to navigate, get the lay of the land, and then get moving.

The Person You're Becoming

The Identity Engine isn't just building the outcome. It's building YOU. The discipline you develop. The resilience you forge. The self-reputation you earn. The identity you construct.

These are all aspects of self that you keep forever.

The short-term outcomes will come and go. Market conditions change. Bodies age. Relationships end. Businesses fail. But the person you become through the Identity Engine? That's yours. It's permanent and transferable across all contexts of life. You don't need external motivation to act. You don't need permission to begin or validation to continue. You don't need perfect conditions to succeed.

You've become the solution to your own problems.

The Truth

The Desert isn't a sign the process is broken. It's where the process actually does its work.
Enthusiasm might get you started, but the Desert is where you find out if you're building something real or just playing at transformation. Most quit here. They're capable of doing the work, they just can't do it without external validation.
If this one hit hard: Chapter 14 (Beliefs Are the Blueprint) is where the invisible rules driving your expectations get examined. Including the belief that if it's working, you should be able to feel it working. Chapter 18 (The Work Evolves. It Never Ends.) is the honest truth about what the long game looks like when the Desert stops being a phase and becomes the practice.

Chapter 6

Confidence Is a Consequence.

THE LIE: Confidence is something you have or you don't. The people who seem to have it were born with it, found it, or faked it into reality.
WHY IT HOLDS: Because you can fake the feeling for a little while and buy a few minutes of borrowed confidence, just long enough to mistake it for the real thing. Then life hits and the performance collapses, because there was never anything underneath it.

You've been taught confidence completely backwards. You've been told it's something you can generate, through affirmations, mirror pep talks and manifesting, even through motivational videos. But all of these are just borrowed and flimsy feelings.

In Chapter 3 we talked about Promise Debt, and why you're likely struggling across so many areas of your life. When you've broken enough commitments to yourself to land in self-bankruptcy, of course you want to believe confidence comes from affirmations instead of actions. When your track record contradicts your potential, you try to hope it into existence instead of committing to a process to develop it. The former is a hack, the latter is a long-term effort.

But confidence isn't a mood. It's not an emotion you summon on command or a mindset you install with the right mantra. Confidence is a consequence. You create it through your choices, your consistency, and your willingness to keep the promises you make to yourself.

You can see the opposite being sold everywhere. Scroll your social feeds, or randomly choose any personal development podcast. Skim book titles on Amazon. Many of the "experts" are selling you confidence like it's a product you can buy or a switch you can flip.

"Fake it till you make it!" "Believe in yourself!" "Manifest your confidence!" It's all bullshit. Self-belief matters, and positive thinking has its place. But they're putting the cart before the horse. Confidence without evidence is just delusion in disguise.

And there's research on this, the kind that stings if you've ever leaned on an affirmation to feel better. Psychologists had people repeat "I'm a lovable person" and measured how they felt afterward. The ones who already had high self-esteem got a small lift. The ones with low self-esteem, the exact people who often turn to affirmations in the first place, felt *worse*. The line collided with everything their track record had already taught them, and their brain hauled up every counterexample to prove it wrong. The affirmation didn't fill the gap. It lit it up.

That's the whole problem in one experiment. You can't affirm your way into confidence when your actions tell a different story. Your subconscious knows the score, and it remembers every broken promise.

Real confidence (the kind that doesn't crumble the moment you face real pressure) isn't built through self-talk. It's built through self-reputation, the record you earn one kept promise at a time. That record is what finally lets you trust yourself, and trust is what confidence stands on.

Your First Promise of the Day

The most important promise you make each day isn't to your spouse, your kids, or your boss. It's the promise you make to yourself about how you'll begin your mornings. The very first actions you take when you wake up.

It's a common story when I first begin working with a new client. They approach their mornings like they approach their lives, reactively. They sleep until the last possible minute, wake up in a panic, grab their phone before their feet hit the floor, and spend the first two hours of their day responding to everyone else's agenda. They start every day in a deficit. Behind. Anxious. And then they wonder why they don't trust themselves to follow through on bigger actions and decisions. I'm not asking you to design better mornings on Canva, or whatever the most recent app promising to organize your life is. We're talking about building a version of you that can be trusted when the stakes in life get real. Because when that happens, you'll either rise to the occasion with certainty or you'll crumble under the pressure. And those consequences can prove severe.

With almost every client I work with, we design their mornings before they go to bed. Not when they wake up feeling motivated (as if they would ever actually feel that way). Not when they're feeling like it. But the night before, when it's a choice and not a reaction.

Our goal is usually to map out the first 30-45 minutes. Wake up. Make the bed. Brush teeth. Wash face. Read something inspiring for fifteen minutes. Walk around the block. We're looking for a combination of actions to give them immediate wins, a term I call win-stacking.

These aren't random productivity hacks. They're promise-keeping practice sessions. Because when you design your morning before you go to bed and then execute it exactly as planned, you're proving something crucial to yourself. That you're someone who does what you say you'll do.

Prove you can keep your word first thing in the morning, and every other challenge you'll face that day feels easier. Think about it this way. The first choice you make every day is either to keep your word to yourself or break it.

Hit snooze instead of getting up when you planned? You've broken your first promise before your feet hit the floor.

Skip the walk you committed to because it's cold outside? You've taught your brain that your comfort matters more than your word.

Each of these might seem small. Insignificant. But they're not. Every one is a small act of telling yourself who you are. Keep the promise and you're someone whose word means something. Break it and you're someone whose word is up for negotiation. Every broken promise, even the tiniest of ones, chips away at your self-trust. Every kept promise builds that feeling back up.

And that design gets tested in the same sixty seconds every day... The ones right after the morning alarm. So let me coach you through the worst rep of the day, the same way I do with my clients.

Start by understanding that there is no decision to make at 6AM. You made it last night, when it was a choice and not a reaction. The you under those warm covers wasn't in that meeting and doesn't get a say now. So when your brain starts presenting its case anyway (it's cold, you're exhausted, ten more minutes changes nothing), recognize the voice. That's your comfort zone negotiating for its life, the same one from the introduction. And you will never out-argue it, because it doesn't need to win. It only needs a delay. So don't argue. Just move. And the move is almost insultingly small... Feet on the floor. That's the entire assignment.

Your body can execute it on zero motivation, and the feeling you've been waiting for (awake, ready, willing) lives on the other side of the move. Stop waiting on the feeling to show up before the move. Your pillow will win every time you do.

Then grab the cheapest win in the house and make the bed. Sixty seconds. Two kept promises posted before the world has asked you for anything, and your old identity has lost almost all of its negotiating power. It knows what you're now learning... **Whoever wins the first promise usually wins the day.**

Because the first hour of your day is about identity, not productivity. The most successful people I've worked with don't start their days hoping to feel confident. They start their day earning confidence through micro-promises they've designed to be achievable but meaningful. Making the bed is about proving you're someone who finishes what you start. The fifteen-minute walk is about proving you're someone who prioritizes your own well-being.

When you stack these wins before the world makes any demands on you, you've begun your day by proving that you're someone capable of leading yourself. You don't need external direction or motivation. You can generate your own, and that's where true personal agency comes from.

For many people, a significant portion of their daily anxiety and self-doubt comes from living out of alignment with their self-made promises. I'm not talking about clinical anxiety disorders. Those are real medical conditions that require professional support. But when you consistently break small commitments to yourself, your nervous system learns not to trust your own word. And when you can't trust yourself, everything feels uncertain and out of control. You become anxious because you've trained your brain to expect self-betrayal.

The people who stay stuck in Promise Debt wake up and immediately start the day in a reactive state. Checking phones, responding to messages, letting other people's priorities dictate their first thoughts and actions. They're anxious throughout the rest of the day because they started the day by abandoning themselves.

When you begin your day by keeping promises to yourself, you're not starting from deficit. You're starting from surplus. From a place of momentum. The confidence you feel is earned. It's a natural consequence of living in alignment with your own true standards.

The Identity Engine Runs on Fuel, Not Fantasy

Remember the Identity Engine from Chapter 5? The system that turns identity into results? It needs fuel to run. And that fuel isn't motivation or positive thinking. It's evidence. Evidence that you follow through. That you can be trusted. That when you commit to becoming someone, you show up as them.

Your morning routine feeds the Identity Engine the proof it needs to keep building the person you're becoming. When the Engine starts its day with clean fuel (kept promises, aligned actions), it runs smoothly all day. When it starts with dirty fuel (broken promises, reactive choices), it sputters and stalls. That breakdown shows up as self-doubt and procrastination, until you can't trust yourself with anything bigger.

I worked with a client named David, who came to me convinced he had a confidence problem. Successful guy on paper, but constantly second-guessing himself and struggling to make decisions. He also had an intense case of imposter syndrome. And all of this self-doubt had plateaued his career long enough that his boss had begun having difficult conversations with him about his future.

After our "getting to know each other" session, the first thing I asked him wasn't about his career or his goals. I asked him about his mornings.

"I usually hit snooze three or four times," he said. "Then I grab my phone and check emails in bed for like twenty minutes and reply to any crises there in my inbox. Then I rush to get ready and grab coffee on the way to work."

"How does that kind of morning make you feel?" I asked.

"Terrible. Like I'm already behind before the day even starts."

That's when I knew we'd likely found the core problem. David didn't have a confidence issue, he had a self-reputation issue. And this problem was being reinforced every single morning, so we redesigned them. Wake up at 6:00. No snooze button or he faced a monetary penalty. Make the bed immediately. Drink a glass of water. Read for fifteen minutes, some of this while brushing his teeth. Quick bodyweight workout to generate some endorphins. Shower. Coffee at home, not on the run. None of this was revolutionary. None of it required special skills or circumstances.

Still, the first week was rough. His body fought him on the wake-up time, and it cost him a hundred bucks to a political cause he hated. And his mind kept trying to negotiate with the plan, but David stuck with it.

By week two, he had begun looking forward to the routine. Those first thirty minutes of the day became his time, his space, his proof that he was becoming someone who could stick to his word.

By week three, the confidence began to show up naturally. He had evidence he was capable, so he no longer had to hope it into existence.

Within a few months he'd made two major career moves he'd been avoiding for years. None of it required massive risk or Instagram bravado. Just clarity, groundedness, and a refusal to keep outsourcing his future to self-doubt. His morning routine had become the foundation for all of it.

The Confidence Equation

The math of confidence is simple. And you already built the first line of it back in Chapter 3, when kept promises started compounding into self-trust.

Kept Promises + Time = Self-Trust

Self-Trust + Evidence = Real Confidence

Real Confidence + Action = Results

But the math doesn't care which inputs you feed it.

Broken Promises + Time = Self-Doubt

Self-Doubt + Avoidance = Anxiety

Anxiety + Inaction = Stagnation

Look at what those equations are really doing. They're closing the gap between the two faces of your Promise Debt account. Self-trust is the feeling. Self-reputation is the record. For all your stuck years they likely disagreed... You felt capable while your ledger said otherwise, or you tried to fake a confidence your personal record couldn't or wouldn't back up. Confidence is what shows up the day they finally match, on the day you've earned it and the feeling catches up to the truth.

Every choice you make feeds one equation or the other. Big or small. Every choice.

This is the behavior loop, written as a formula. Behavior sits on the left of every line. Belief sits on the right. Each kept promise hands the belief layer a piece of evidence it can't argue with, and confidence is the name for what happens when enough of that evidence stacks up and the belief finally updates to match. You out-prove your way there, one promise at a time.

The promise you make to wake up at a certain time. The goal to move your body. The decision to read something meaningful instead of scrolling mindlessly. The choice to prepare your mind before you engage with the world's demands. These are all so much more than just habits. They're the raw materials of self-trust, and that keeps you moving. And then self-reputation is something you build through the accumulated evidence of your own reliability.

When the Identity Engine runs consistently on this kind of fuel, confidence stops being something you have to think about. Instead, it becomes something you embody.

Because real confidence isn't loud. It doesn't need to announce itself or prove anything to anyone. It's quiet certainty. It's the calm that comes from knowing that when you say you'll do something, you'll do it. It's the peace that comes from living in alignment with your own standards.

Confidence is the natural byproduct of a person who has trained themselves to be trustworthy, especially to themselves. And it begins with something as seemingly simple as keeping your word about when you'll wake up tomorrow.

CHALLENGE

Tonight, before you go to bed, design tomorrow morning. Write down exactly what you'll do in the first 20-30 minutes after you wake up. Be specific, and be honest about what you're actually willing to commit to. I'll take two honest actions over eight empty aspirations, any day of the week.

Then do it. Exactly as planned. The convenience doesn't matter. How you feel doesn't matter. You said you would do it.

Try this out for seven days and watch what happens to your relationship with yourself.

The Truth

Every kept promise is a deposit. Every broken one is a withdrawal. Your subconscious has been keeping that ledger your whole life, and it doesn't lie. Even when you're willing to lie to yourself.

You don't deserve confidence because you want it. You earn it because you showed up when you didn't feel like it, kept the promise no one else would have known you broke, and did it again the next day.

Confidence isn't a feeling you manufacture. It's a consequence you create.

If this one hit hard: Chapter 13 (Borrowed Identity Always Breaks) is where the confidence you've been performing (built on external validation instead of internal evidence) finally gets examined. Chapter 14 (Beliefs Are the Blueprint) gets into the invisible architecture underneath your defaults, including the beliefs about yourself that made borrowed confidence feel like the only option.

MINI: Everyone's a Guru Until They Get Punched in the Teeth.

Everyone's a guru until they get punched in the teeth.

Sunday night, you're basically performing your own TED Talk. You're watching documentaries about greatness, reading books about billionaire habits, and planning your world domination like you've got a personal board of directors cheering you on.

You're mapping out your perfect morning routine (meditation, journaling, cold shower, obviously). You're setting intentions that would make Oprah weep. You're basically one repeated mantra away from nirvana-levels of enlightenment...

Then Monday morning arrives and you're hitting the snooze button like it owes you money.

By 10AM, you're drowning in emails and wondering why your revolutionary insights from last night feel about as practical as bringing a vision board to a knife fight. By 5PM, you're back to scrolling through motivational Instagram posts, looking for the next hit of wisdom that'll definitely stick this time. By Tuesday, you've forgotten most of what EVER inspired you.

And the cycle continues. Your addiction to motivation porn grows. And somehow you never notice that you've become a connoisseur of transformation content but a complete failure at real transformation.

So... How many of the challenges in this book have you completed? Not skimmed. Not "meant to do." But really done? Like, from beginning to end. Go ahead and count them. I'll wait.

If you're reading this book like most people consume self-help content, then you've magically absorbed every insight, nodded along with every truth... And avoided most of the actual work. You've turned this book into sophisticated procrastination disguised as personal development.

Look, I get it. Challenges feel like homework. They interrupt your flow of consumption. And they're also kind of uncomfortable. I know, I designed them. They force you to confront the gap between what you know and what you do.

Content consumption without execution is just self-deception with really great PR. I learned this the hard way, during my own addiction to motivation porn. Every insight you collect but never apply becomes another piece of evidence that you're someone who knows what to do but doesn't do it. And every chapter of this book you finish without acting on it reinforces the identity you're trying to escape.

You didn't pick up this book to become a more informed person. At least, I hope you didn't. It does have a great cover... But, no. You picked it up to become a different person. And different people do different things, especially when they don't feel like it. Because they've stopped waiting to feel motivated. Motivation was never meant to be stockpiled like a precious resource. It's meant to be used up, converted into action the moment it shows up. Treat inspiration as a substitute for implementation, and you're building an addiction to potential rather than progress.

That's what motivation porn does to you. It floods your brain with the rewards of (perceived) progress without requiring any of the actual work. You watch the documentary and feel like you learned something. You read the book and feel like you've grown. But feeling isn't doing, and doing is the only thing that counts.

This addiction makes you feel productive while keeping you paralyzed. You're so busy consuming knowledge that you never take the time to act on it. You collect strategies you'll never use and study philosophies you'll never live.

Paradoxically, the smarter you are, the more susceptible you are to this trap. Smart people love complexity. They love nuance and the feeling of understanding something deeply. Before you know it, you're three books deep into someone's recommended reading list and two podcasts into their interview circuit. And you've confused learning about success with committing to the actions that truly build success.

The person who reads one business book and starts a company will always beat the person who reads fifty business books and starts nothing.

Action beats analysis. Every single time.

Before you read another word, go back and pick one challenge you skipped. The one that made you think "I should do that" before you kept reading. Do it now. Not when you finish the book. Right. Fucking. Now.

Because the distance between knowing and doing is where dreams go to die. And if you can't close that gap in a book designed to help you do that very thing, what makes you think you'll close it once you're plugged back into real life?

Everyone's a guru until they get punched in the teeth. Anyone can be a philosopher until they're tired, behind, and afraid.

That's when you find out who you really are. And that's when your future is determined.

Day One

Be real. Have you been skipping the challenges?

I literally called you out for it in the MINI a moment ago. If you have done the challenges, rock on. All good if you want to just skip over to Chapter 7.

But if you're consuming and not doing, then we need to have a word. That gap between learning and action is exactly what this book is about. And you've been living it in real time. If you just keep powering on and reading the book, but then never actually change anything? I'm keeping it real with you, as I promised I would. You'll have wasted your time. And we both know it.

If you know you need support in executing the challenges in this book (and more), then I've designed a program to do just that. It's called Day One. Twenty-one days of emails, lessons, and videos built to hold you accountable for breaking the lies and clearing your Promise Debt, one day at a time.

You don't need more inspiration. We've established that. But if needed, I can help you close that action gap and keep you from sliding further back into consumption mode.

21 Days. One email a day. All implementation.

The book has everything you need. **Day One** makes sure you actually use it.

Chapter 7

No One's Coming to Film YOUR Montage.

THE LIE: Real transformation is built on breakthroughs. The right decision in the right moment, getting the right mentor. You hit it big, and then you become someone different.
WHY IT HOLDS: Because that's the only transformation story anyone ever tells. Nobody posts about the 47th consecutive morning they showed up before anyone else was awake. You only see the highlight. So it makes sense to just keep waiting for yours.

Everyone wants to live the montage moment.

You know the scene. The music kicks in and the hero transforms through pure grit and relentless repetition. Rocky sprinting up the Philadelphia stairs. The Karate Kid mastering his craft through endless chores. Neo sparring with Morpheus in the digital dojo. Almost any shonen anime ever.

We love watching these sequences because they condense months of unglamorous work into a few inspiring minutes, making the transformation feel almost inevitable. Especially when it's set to a rocking soundtrack.

But... Here you are in the real world, waiting for someone else to write your montage instead of filming it yourself.

You've learned that confidence comes from consequences, and that Promise Debt destroys self-reputation. You've stopped waiting for someone else to save you. Now comes the practical question, though. How do you actually build the person capable of holding the life you want?

The answer isn't Instagrammable, and in real life that banging soundtrack is nowhere to be found. There are zero guarantees your hard work will ever pay off. All that's waiting on you are repetition, sweat, silence, and the discipline to keep "filming" your grind while no one's watching.

That's the montage no one wants to make. But it's the only one that actually works.

The Heroes We Love vs. The Lives We Live

Think about your favorite transformation story. I'd be willing to bet this book's royalties that there's a training montage in there somewhere. You know, that sequence where the protagonist becomes someone new through raw eggs and sheer determination.

We love these sequences because they show us what's possible. Not sure if you've ever thought about it, but from the hero's perspective they have no clue they're quite literally in a montage. They're just training, putting in rep after rep. And most crucially, they're doing it (from their perspective) when there's no music playing, no cameras rolling, and no guarantee it will ever pay off.

There were no highlight reels when a sophomore Michael Jordan failed to make his high school's varsity team. But what did he do next? He arrived at school before the rest of his town was awake, just so he could practice for hours before classes started. He spent the day sweaty and exhausted, but didn't care. And he did this for 365 days straight, his only focus on fundamentals such as footwork and shooting with his left hand. The following year he not only made his high school team, but also became the star and was recruited to play for one of the greatest college coaches of his era.

That's a real-life training montage. And it's the exact opposite of how most people approach change. They want the victory scene without the sweat, and the transformation without the discomfort.

But you can't have it both ways. You don't get to skip the middle and still have an ending worth filming.

The Cost of Disconnecting

I watch this play out constantly in my coaching practice. People who had a few breakout years and found big success, only to hit a wall that brought their career to a screeching halt. The talent was still there, but they'd lost the willingness to train like they still had something to prove.

So they reach out to me, utterly frustrated with their place in life. "I don't get it. I'm doing the same things, but it's just not clicking."

That's the lie. And deep down, they know it.

What they're really doing is clinging to past victories while knowingly skipping the foundational work that built their past successes. The early morning prospecting blocks? No longer on the calendar. The detailed call prep? Occasionally considered, never done. The relentless ownership of pipeline movement? Replaced by hope.

These people had a training montage and experienced some highlights, but then they stepped away from the sequence. Many of them for years. They're not necessarily broken, but they're lost.

The first step in any change process is awareness. So we examine what made them elite in the past. It's usually some form of relentless commitment to the boring, but critical, inputs for their job that compounded over time into big results. Then I challenge them to imagine the next peak, something even higher than their previous run, and I ask them to consider what the daily repetitions would need to look like to earn that. The response I get almost every single time? It's nearly identical to that past process they had committed to previously.

For you, what would that version of training look like? What are the reps you've been actively skipping?

That's where the real work begins.

If I told you I've been crushing these training montages for years, I'd be full of shit. Instead, I'll build a waiting list of clients and rationalize that as a reason to ease up on the networking I've openly admitted to hating (social anxiety). Several months later I've worked through the wait list... And I haven't gotten a new referral in months. Should I be surprised? I knew what to do the whole time. I just stopped doing it when no one was around to hold me accountable and there was nothing urgent forcing me to. Working the process in the quiet, with no applause and no guarantee? That's freaking hard. It never stops being hard. But it's what's required.

Nothing but you and the Groundhog Day of greatness you know is required for your success. If you're in sales, it might look like:

90 Minutes of outbound calls while others are checking emails or scrolling their socials.

Prepping for every meeting like it's Game 7 of the NBA Finals.

Tracking where every deal sits and designing the next nudge to get it moving again. Every day.

Getting rejected 9 times and showing up with enthusiasm for the 10th ask.

At first, my clients complain. They drag their heels for a week or two, perpetually stuck in first gear. The dopamine is nowhere to be found.

By week 3, breakthrough moments begin to appear.

They finally do some serious prep and walk into a sales meeting ready to rock it. And, sure enough, they close with precision. A prospect who's been circling for months suddenly says yes to a meaningful nudge. Their calendar fills up after following through on 10 straight mornings of outbound blocks. The deals start stacking. They feel it. They're back in the rhythm.

No shortcuts. No secret sauce. Just relentless focus on putting in rep after rep. Designing intentional blocks of action and living them on loop.

A few months in, they look up from their pipeline, half-drained after another day of rinse-and-repeat... And it clicks. They've built something awesome, a system that works when they work it. A pipeline of future wins they no longer have to chase, because their discipline built the gravity necessary to pull their successes to them.

I saw this same pattern with a client who was rebuilding her life after a grueling divorce. She was wiped, and she had long ago stopped caring about herself. We spent a couple of sessions designing her non-negotiable routine for self-care. There were daily workouts, meal planning with a nutritionist, yoga sessions for restoration, and even biweekly spa sessions (I've never seen anyone have to get dragged to a spa, but here we were). She had spent so much time being selfless, she'd forgotten how to be positively selfish. And we had a hard commitment this journey was hers and no one else's, so this area of her life was off limits from social media. This was her training montage for film, in quiet. She never won an award for this period of time. But she did ultimately build a life she actually wanted to live within, one rep at a time.

This is when my clients realize something the highlight reel never shows. **The grind wasn't a sacrifice. It was an investment. The statue doesn't reveal itself to the artist after one swing of the hammer... It comes from ten thousand intentional blows made over time.**

That's a training montage. And every one of us has to write our own.

Why Most Montages Die Before They Ever Begin

Most of the sabotage happens before the cameras start rolling. People redesign the plan every week instead of sticking to the reps, or they constantly hunt for novelty instead of honoring repetition. They open their social feeds and begin comparing their daily inputs to someone else's highlight reel and decide they're doing it wrong, so they try to "optimize" their system before they even have enough data to decide it works. They quit too early because it doesn't feel worthy of posting on their Facebook feed.

And don't confuse filming your montage with perfect execution. That's unrealistic and demoralizing. Your focus should be on nothing but persistent execution. It's about showing up on the days when showing up feels pointless. It's about trusting the process even when the process feels broken.

Because what most people are really addicted to is the launch, not the work. They get fired up about an idea, spend weeks planning and dreaming... Then hit the wall every builder hits, that long, boring middle. Because that's where the applause fades and the doubt creeps in.

And that's when they bail.

But every story has a middle. And in the middle, everything kind of sucks. No one cheers, even your closest friends. The pace drags. This is where many decide the story they say they want isn't worth the effort it demands. But in every great story (and every great life) the middle is where the transformation happens. It's where the hero earns the right to the moment they claimed to want all along.

Kobe Bryant understood this better than most athletes. His philosophy was simple, "Rest at the end, not in the middle." While other players took plays off during practice, Kobe was notorious for treating every drill like it alone would earn another championship. The middle was where he separated himself from everyone else who was remotely close to him in talent.

The Middle

You feel like nothing's working even though you're working. You've stopped getting external praise for your efforts. The novelty wore off months ago, and now it's just you, your discipline, and the monotonous repetition you committed to. You're tempted to burn it all down and start over with something that feels more exciting. You keep fantasizing about quitting or pivoting to a different approach. You wonder if you're wasting your time on something that will never pay off.

Welcome to the middle. Keep working.

And if this terrain feels familiar, it should. You're standing in the Desert from Chapter 5. Same silence, same invisible progress, same negotiation with quitting. You named this place forty pages ago. Now you're living in it. This is the bail-out point. But it's also where the montage actually happens. This is where the hero is forged, and it happens when questioning the process feels most valid and when your doubts sure feel like their arguments are carrying the greatest amount of logic yet.

The middle doesn't feel like progress because progress is compounded over time, it's exponential in nature. It builds quietly, invisibly, until one day you realize you've become someone who can handle things that used to break you. And the exponential curve of explosive personal growth and results kicks in right towards the end of that brutal middle period. This is when Neo has mastered kung fu and is ready for his first critical mission. When the Karate Kid has realized he's learned the Miyagi style and is ready for the tournament.

Think about the greatest athletes, leaders, and innovators of our time. They obsess over the fundamentals. They embrace the boring and fall in love with the process.

Before Spanx ever became a national brand, Sara Blakely invested two years testing prototypes and being rejected by manufacturers before landing her first big break. She spent her evenings calling manufacturers from her apartment, getting hung up on repeatedly, then calling the next name on her list. James Clear didn't just write a bestseller in *Atomic Habits*, he wrote one article every Monday and Thursday for three years. Same schedule, same commitment, whether 10 people read it or 10,000. These were systems, not occasional bursts of effort when they felt like it. Daily practices that became identity. And these aren't just success stories. They're montages that all share one thing in common, and that's the willingness to do repetitive work consistently.

And let me be as clear as possible about a critical point around this topic. This isn't toxic hustle culture disguised as transformation advice. The montage is about choosing scenes with purpose, and about persistence through the unglamorous middle. It's identity-aligned, with a focus on the daily practice of becoming someone who can hold the life you actually want.

Write Your Own Montage

No one is coming to rescue you from an uninspiring story, nor is anyone going to hand you the transformation you haven't earned. And I can promise you no one is coming to roll the cameras if you haven't given them something worth filming.

You're not the audience. You're the screenwriter. And every screenwriter lives by one rule... No boring scenes without purpose.

You are holding the pen right now. So think progression and perseverance, not perfection. You don't need a life that looks good on social media. You need a plan that makes you feel alive and that drives you forward in the direction of your choosing.

Screenwriter's Rule: If the scene you're living today doesn't belong in your highlight reel, rewrite it. Not later. Right now.

Montage Reality Check: If a film crew followed you for 30 days, would they have enough footage to make a montage? If not, then let's design some damn scenes worthy of an 80s power ballad and get to filming them.

The montage isn't optional. Only the one who writes it is.

And remember, a training montage isn't a perfect, linear progression of wins. It includes failures, plateaus, and moments of doubt. **What makes it powerful is the persistence through struggle, not the absence of struggle.**

"Rest at the end, not in the middle. Have a dream, sacrifice for it, and never, ever, rest in the middle." — Kobe Bryant, 2016

The Truth

Nobody's coming to film your montage. No crowd, no music, no guarantee the work pays off. Just the reps you do when no one's watching and nothing feels like progress.

That's not a problem with the process. *That is the fucking process.*

The grind isn't the sacrifice you make to get to the good part. It is the good part. The one that actually builds the person capable of holding what comes next.

If this one hit hard: Chapter 12 (This Is Where You Always Quit) is about the pattern of abandoning the work right when the boring middle feels most permanent. Chapter 18 (The Work Evolves. It Never Ends.) is where the longer truth lives, that the montage doesn't stop, it just changes shape.

Chapter 8

You're Not Confused. You're Scared.

THE LIE: You're not avoiding anything. You just need to understand the situation better before you commit to a direction. Once it's clear, the right move will be obvious.
WHY IT HOLDS: Because analysis feels responsible. Research feels like preparation. Asking for more opinions feels like due diligence. None of it feels like fear... Which is exactly what makes it so effective as a hiding place.

You've been "thinking about X" for months. X meaning any of 26 different things in your life.

You've googled "how to know if it's the right time" more than you'd care to admit. You've asked way too many friends for advice that you already know you won't take. You've made pros and cons lists, consulted your journal. You maybe even pulled some cards from that tarot deck you bought during your last identity crisis.

Meanwhile, the opportunities are slipping away while you "perfect" your approach to something that only requires you to hit send.

You can write the perfect training montage, visualize every scene, plan every detail. But if you never actually start filming, you're just another person with a "perfect" script they're too scared to film. The antidote to overthinking isn't more thinking (or planning or preparation).

It's movement.

You think the struggle is not knowing what to do. It's not, though. The struggle is doing it when the conditions don't feel perfect for beginning. So you wait. You wait for clarity or for confidence. You wait for someone to tell you it's okay. Or even worse, you wait until the fear goes away.

Action is the antidote. Not certainty. Not planning. Not journaling. Action.

Most people fail because they made no decision, not because they made the wrong decision.

They waited. And waited. And then they overthought some more. They ended up stuck (often for years) because they believed clarity would come before movement.

Underneath the stall is a question very few stop to ask. Who's making this call? Because there are two of you in the room. The one you're building toward, who already knows what this requires. And the scared one from yesterday, who just wants the discomfort to stop. Right now the scared one has been running your decisions, which is exactly why your efforts at change have failed. We'll come back to this. For now, just notice which one of those two is in the driver's seat.

Why Your Brain Wants You to Stay Stuck

One of the hardest truths I've had to learn? The people who stay stuck aren't lazy. They're terrified, and they're just listening to the wrong voice. Your brain tells you that if you wait a little longer or research a little more, that the fear will go away. That clarity will arrive like a lightning bolt. That the "right" moment will announce itself.

And that's all bullshit.

I know this pattern from the inside. After my conversation with Pennee, I submitted my resignation. Clean decision, right? I was finally doing it, making a huge bet on myself. Except... I promised to stay through the end of the Fall semester. Very reasonable since education runs on semesters, so it would be a clean transition point for everyone. So I spent those months doing hundreds of hours of research on what professional coaching looked like. I just never actually coached anyone. And then December arrived and I was offered a New Schools Coach role. Six-month term, open a handful of schools, good salary. It even had "coach" in the title. I told myself it would help me prepare. Even though, of course, I already had mountains of evidence I could coach, mentor, and consult. None of that mattered. What did matter was the cool coach title came with a paycheck and a reason to wait. So I took it. Pennee eventually put her foot down again, and understandably so. Way too much travel meant my runway was up and it was time to shoot my shot. The decision I'd made in the garage took almost a year to act on, because fear doesn't disappear after a big moment. It just finds a new job title to hide behind.

Because your mind isn't trying to help you succeed. It's trying to keep you safe. And safe feels like staying exactly where you are, even when where you are is slowly killing you. So you'll tell yourself that you're confused. But you're not confused, you're scared. You're scared that moving forward means giving up the familiar, even when the familiar isn't working. You're scared of being wrong. You're scared of the work that comes after the decision. So you hide in analysis. You disguise avoidance as wisdom. You mistake planning for progress.

And you know exactly what I'm talking about.

Changing your LinkedIn headline ten times instead of applying for the job.

Researching business plans instead of talking to even just one potential customer.

Reading relationship advice instead of having the difficult conversation with your partner.

Watching YouTube videos about fitness instead of, you know, going to the gym.

The pattern is always the same. People trade short-term comfort for long-term regret. They swap action for analysis. Most people don't even realize they're overthinking because it feels productive. But analysis paralysis has tells, and once you know them you can catch yourself in the act.

Asking for opinions from people who've never faced your situation.

Needing just one more piece of information before committing to a decision.

Planning your planning sessions. Yes, this is a real thing and it's very common. You're likely doing it as well.

If you're doing any of these, you're not being thorough. You're avoiding.

Make the Call, Then Make It Right

I once worked with a couple who came to me overwhelmed by stress and constant fighting. They had all the symptoms of a relationship in full-blown crisis. Resentment, exhaustion, and that dead look in the eyes that comes from years of unresolved conflict. But it didn't take long to realize the real problem wasn't communication skills or date nights. The lie they were telling themselves was simple. "We don't know what to do."

But the truth was harder, as it often is for all of us. They knew exactly what they needed to do. They were just terrified to do it.

After weeks of brutally honest sessions, they reached a conclusion that left them reeling. Their marriage was over. They still loved each other. But staying together was destroying both of them and their kids. Most couples would sit on that realization for months. They'd get more opinions. They'd hope it would somehow fix itself. Not these two. The choice they made was clear. They looked at each other and said, "If we're doing this, we're doing it right."

The cost they paid was real. Divorce. Rebuilding their identities. Massive uncertainty about their future. And mostly, the pain of telling their children.

But the transformation they earned was worth it. Within a handful of months, they had become better parents apart than they ever were together. She finally launched the business she'd been dreaming of. He built boundaries at work and became a leader people wanted to follow. Their kids? They're thriving, because their parents owned the aftermath. Hell yes they still have difficult days and have to navigate disagreements. But they put in the effort to build a system they could co-parent around, and they stick to it no matter what.

Today, they are legit best friends. They co-parent beautifully. And they both credit the same thing. They didn't wait for the "right time" to pull the trigger on their divorce. They moved. And then they put all of their resources into making the difficult decision the right decision.

This is the secret that the chronically stuck miss. **The initial decision is rarely what defines the outcome. It's what you do after the decision that shapes everything.**

Avoidance Is the Real Enemy

Fear isn't the enemy. It's a signal.

Avoidance is the enemy. Because avoidance rewires your brain to retreat from the very life you say you want.

We avoid hard conversations. We avoid choosing. We avoid action by hiding in "productivity"... Making lists, reading more books, asking for more time, waiting for more signs.

Avoidance feels safe in the short term, and the relief is real. That's the trap.

The second you dodge the thing you're scared of, the anxiety drops, your brain files that relief away as a reward, and it learns to reach for avoidance again next time. Psychologists call it negative reinforcement, and it's the same loop the most effective anxiety treatments are built to break. But you're only borrowing that relief. The thing that calms you down now is the same thing teaching your brain the threat was real, so the fear never shrinks. It compounds.

Every time you avoid action, you reinforce the belief that you're not capable. You damage your self-reputation, and you train your brain to believe that discomfort is a stop sign, not a green light. Every hour you wait, you're not holding steady. You're making a withdrawal. The decision you keep ducking doesn't sit there neutral, it posts to the ledger as one more piece of evidence that your own word doesn't move you. That's the part avoidance hides. You think you're protecting yourself from the risk of a wrong call. But instead, you're actually spending your self-reputation with yourself to do it, and that bill comes due with interest.

This is why so many people hate their jobs but never leave. It's why relationships drag on long after they should end. It's why dream businesses remain perpetually "almost ready to launch." It's why health goals get recycled year after year.

Avoidance is the silent killer of potential. And it masquerades as wisdom and patience.

Fear Doesn't Disappear Before Action

People think they need to feel ready before they act. Nope. That's a lie, and believing it hands control of your life over to your fear.

You'll wait forever for a fear-free moment, because the truth is different. Fear fades after movement, not before it. You take one hard step... And your truth shifts along with your new perspective. The story in your head changes and your body begins to regulate itself. Your brain says, "Oh, we're doing this. I guess we're okay."

Action interrupts the fear loop.

This is biology, not mindset fluff. Action changes your physiology. The moment you do the thing you've been avoiding, your body gets evidence that the threat wasn't what it feared, and your nervous system slowly updates its association with it. That's not a feeling. It's the same extinction process that real anxiety treatment runs on. Even a small, tangential action starts loosening fear's grip, because fear feeds on stillness.

That's why doing something (even if it's not "the thing") can lead to a breakthrough. Schedule the meeting you've been putting off. Make the call you keep somehow finding a reason to not make. The action doesn't have to be the whole leap, but it has to at least point at the thing you're avoiding. Not away from it.

Action starves fear.

You already know this move, by the way. It's the same one that got you out of bed in Chapter 6. **The body goes first and the feeling arrives after, whether the rep is feet on the floor or fingers dialing the number.** Same move. Heavier weight.

I work with founders who face this reality every day. One client had developed an offering they knew would disrupt their industry, but kept delaying the launch. We talked for weeks about his fears: rejection, criticism, failure. But the fear didn't budge until he took the smallest action. He called one potential customer. Just one.

The call went well. Then he booked another. Then another.

Within a month, he had pre-sold enough to cover his initial production run. The fear didn't disappear before he acted, it fled because he acted.

Your brain needs evidence, not encouragement. And action is the only way to get it. Because once you start moving, everything gets easier. Not sure if you remember this from college physics, but a body at rest stays at rest, and a body in motion stays in motion. The hardest part isn't staying in motion. It's breaking the stillness in the first place. That first push, from zero to moving, takes the most out of you. After that, momentum does some of the work for you, and your brain starts expecting action instead of analysis.

Momentum builds upon itself.

It compounds through repetitive alignment. When you do the hard thing you said you'd do, again and again, your brain starts to believe you. One bold action makes the next one significantly easier. You start building evidence that you can do hard things. That you do follow through, even when it's messy or scary.

Most People Wait Forever for Certainty

The most successful people I coach don't spend time chasing the "right" decision.

They get to 70% certainty, and then they freaking go. And once they're in motion they course correct as needed, adapting and taking responsibility for the outcome. Whatever comes, their energy is focused on improving as they go. They don't waste their life hoping for a map. They build the terrain with their steps. Instead of waiting on it, they *create* clarity by moving forward.

I've worked with C-suite executives who made million-dollar decisions with less information than most people require to change their morning commute. They've trained themselves to make decisions differently. **They know that certainty is created, not discovered.** They've built the confidence to say, "I don't know if this is right, but it's the best call I can make with what I know right now. Let's move, and I'll own the outcome."

This is about ownership for your journey. And it's a superpower in a world paralyzed by the fear of being wrong.

Look, I can keep giving you examples all day. I can tell you story after story about people who changed their lives the moment they stopped waiting for permission. But at some point, you have to close this book and do the thing you know you need to do. You know what decision or what tough conversation you've been avoiding. You know what action you've been postponing until "the right time."

Yes, the right time was months ago. The second-best time is now.

You don't have all the answers? So what. You'll never have "all the answers." And waiting is just another form of hiding.

Every day you avoid action is another day you tell yourself, "I'm not ready. I'm not capable. I need more before I can start." And your self-reputation sinks further.

CHALLENGE

Write down the decision you've been avoiding. Don't overthink it. You already know what it is.

Take one action today, something that takes 5-10 minutes at the most. Make the phone call. Buy the URL you've been agonizing over for your side-hustle. Just get in motion.

Kill the story. Whatever excuse you've been using to justify the delay, write it down and cross it out. Physically do this.

Own the outcome. Whatever happens next, you're going to make it work because that's what people who move forward do.

You already have everything you need to take the next step.

Quit reading and go handle your business.

The Truth

You're not confused. You're scared. And there's nothing wrong with being scared, except when you're attempting to label it as something else and using it as an excuse.

Clarity doesn't come before movement. It comes because of it. Every decision you've been waiting to feel ready for was always going to feel exactly like this. Uncertain, uncomfortable, and overdue.

The delay is always more expensive than you think. While you're waiting for the right moment, your self-reputation is paying the price.

If this one hit hard: Chapter 14 (Beliefs Are the Blueprint) gets into the invisible architecture keeping you in analysis mode. Chapter 16 (You Can't Win the Game If You're Playing the Wrong Role) is about showing up as the version of yourself that moves, not the one waiting for permission.

Chapter 9

Balance Is a Lie. Choose Your Sacrifices.

THE LIE: You just need to get better at juggling. The people who have what you want figured out how to do it all (career, health, relationships, growth) without dropping anything. Life balance is the goal.
WHY IT HOLDS: Because the people selling this falsehood will never show you their actual calendar. You're comparing your reality to someone else's Instagram account and calling the gap a personal failure.

You're exhausted. Like feeling it in your bones, totally fucking exhausted.

All of the action you took wasn't wrong. It's tough to ever find a case where just moving forward is ever a bad choice. But the problem is you've been trying to act on EVERYTHING simultaneously. You finally stopped waiting for the perfect moment, and now you're saying yes to every moment. Every opportunity or demand. Every seeming priority.

Each morning, you wake up believing you can have it all and be everything to everyone... And somehow still have energy left for yourself. That delusion is the real cause of your exhaustion. It doesn't slow you down. It speeds you up, straight toward burnout.

When people tell you to just move forward, they don't also explain that you need to choose a direction. Hell, if you only read Chapter 8 from this book then even I would be guilty of this. But choosing that one direction means saying no to ten others. Because you've been sold a fantasy. A well-lit Facebook reel where someone explains how they "do it all." A productivity guru promising you can have every dream without sacrifice.

Balance is a lie.

Not a partial lie. Not a sometimes-lie. But a complete fabrication designed to make you feel inadequate while chasing something that doesn't exist.

You cannot balance your career, relationships, health, spirituality, finances, and personal growth simultaneously at their highest levels. The math of time and energy doesn't work and the physics of attention doesn't allow it. What you can do (what you must do if you want any shot at an extraordinary life) is make deliberate, intentional tradeoffs. Strategic sacrifices. Clear-eyed decisions about what matters most in this season of your life, and what can wait.

I'm not asking you to lower your standards, I'm asking you to focus your resources on what matters most right now. To become incredibly intentional about what you say yes to. Because you cannot say yes to everything while also succeeding at anything.

The Balance Delusion

Think about what people mean when they talk about "work-life balance." They're picturing a perfectly distributed life where nothing important ever gets short-changed. They imagine being the Employee of the Month while also being Parent of the Year, all while maintaining a marriage that makes people jealous AND staying in the best shape of their lives. It sounds beautiful. Hell, it might even sound reasonable to your delusionally hopeful self.

But it's neither.

What this fantasy overlooks is the fundamental reality of human attention and energy... They're both finite and precious.

The balance obsession isn't just misguided, it's addictive. Because as long as you're chasing perfect balance you'll never have to make hard choices. You can stay comfortable in the crossover space between dreams and reality, between wanting and doing. And in the process balance becomes the perfect excuse for mediocrity. "I can't go all-in on my business because I need work-life balance." "I can't transform my body, that would require too much energy from work and family (balance)." Every meaningful goal gets neutered by the balance caveat. This is exactly why most people's lives feel flat. They're not failing spectacularly, they're succeeding at nothing in particular. Their energy is distributed so widely across competing priorities that nothing gets the concentrated attention required for real, meaningful progress. They're living in the gray zone between satisfaction and regret, and they're dressing it up as wisdom.

The balance addiction gives you permission to avoid the discomfort of choice. It lets you hedge every bet, pursue every option half-heartedly, and then blame "life's complexity" when nothing extraordinary emerges from your efforts.

But balance addicts love to avoid a painful truth, that the most fulfilled people they know aren't balanced. They're obsessed. They've chosen what matters most, and they've organized their entire existence around protecting and advancing those priorities. They've accepted that going all-in on one or two things means letting the rest run on maintenance. Sometimes letting a few slide entirely, at least for a season.

I had a client recently, a business owner named Sarah with two kids under five, who came to our first session completely fried. Dark circles under her eyes, apologizing for being ten minutes late because of a daycare situation.

"I don't know what's wrong with me," Sarah said. "Everyone else seems to have this figured out. I see these other moms crushing it in business while still being present for their kids, staying in shape, and keeping their marriages strong. I feel like I'm barely keeping my head above water."

I stopped her right there.

"Show me these women who are crushing it everywhere simultaneously," I said. "Not their LinkedIn posts or their Instagram stories. Show me their actual calendar. Their bank account. Their marriage when the cameras are off. Their energy levels at 9PM."

She couldn't, of course. Because the women she was comparing herself to weren't real, they were highlight reels masquerading as complete documentaries.

Sarah got quiet. After a handful of uncomfortable beats, I told her, "Nobody, and I mean nobody, is giving 100% to everything that matters simultaneously. For the people genuinely doing great in key areas of life, **what looks like balance from the outside is actually strategic prioritization.**"

Sarah's breakthrough started with accepting the thing she's been dodging for years, that meaningful lives require meaningful choices.

Tradeoffs Are Proof Your Life Matters.

Most people resist the idea of tradeoffs because they've been conditioned to believe wanting everything is ambitious and choosing anything is settling. But tradeoffs aren't a punishment. They're the proof that your life actually matters. Because anything meaningful costs something. Every time you say "yes" to something, you're saying "no" to something else. This is about consequences, it's math. Actually, it's a fucking law of the universe. There's a cost to everything, and pretending otherwise is delusional.

The people who build extraordinary things make tradeoffs. They accept that pursuing excellence in one area means temporary sacrifice in others. They know that seasons exist for a reason. The most successful people I've worked with aren't those who find magical harmony between competing priorities. They're the ones who get brutally honest about what matters most right now, and then align their time, energy, and identity around those choices.

You want to build a business that changes your family's financial future? Then you probably won't be training for a marathon at the same time. Or even a 5K.

You want to be deeply present for your kids during a critical developmental stage? Then your career might maintain rather than accelerate for a while.

You want to heal from trauma or rebuild your health? Then some of your bigger professional ambitions might need to take a temporary backseat.

None of these decisions mean that you're a failure. They're strategic choices that acknowledge the realistic flow of life, rather than deluding you in an attempt to swim upstream against it.

Winners Choose Their Losses

Winning at the highest levels is all about choosing which losses you can accept within this season of your life. And this is exactly what separates the people who win from everyone else. **Most will try to avoid any losses at all, while the ones who win deliberately choose where they're willing to take a hit.** They know that trying to win at everything means winning at nothing.

I worked with a director at a tech company who was pulling down good money, but he had this side business idea that was eating at him. And he also had two young kids, a wife climbing the corporate ladder, a mortgage in an expensive city... And on and on. It was nuts. Yeah, he was even trying to compete in Ironman events (and placing in them). He kept telling me he wanted to "find balance" between his day job, his startup dreams, his family, and staying in good physical shape. In turn, I felt morally obligated to be as direct as possible with him. "You're not going to find balance. At some point you're going to have to make choices that hurt."

We got real about what an 18-month launch window would actually cost. First, I asked him what wild success would look like if he had nothing to worry about other than his launch, which we wrote down in great detail. Then I had him make a list of everything he'd have to sacrifice to make that a reality. No more all day training sessions on the weekend, just running and bodyweight stuff at home. Late nights would be replaced with early mornings. The kids' birthday parties would be simpler. He'd have to focus on maintaining his marriage, not trying to perfect it.

His wife wasn't thrilled about some of it, but she respected the honesty and the timeline. Because most couples miss the fact that pretending you can do everything well all at the same time is dishonesty. It's promising your family a version of you that doesn't exist, while delivering a stressed and distracted one that disappoints everyone due to false expectations.

They both knew what they were signing up for, and more importantly, when it would end.

The moment when everything clicked for him? He was at his daughter's soccer game while halfway through his launch phase, watching her play while other dads were checking emails. He realized he wasn't sacrificing his family for his business, he was building something that would give him more time with them in the future. And because this soccer game was an intentionally chosen priority through the lens of opportunity costs, he was truly there and present for her.

The whole concept of tradeoffs suddenly made sense in his soul and not just in his head. Did he make it to crossfit that morning? Nope. Had he had a "guys weekend" that year? Nope. But his launch was going great and he was there for his daughter, sitting with the rest of his family, and he was every bit present in that moment.

The entire family got on board because they understood this was a unified sacrifice for a specific season, not a permanent way of living. And he wasn't hiding anything from them. They were partners in his sacrifice instead of collateral damage.

The result? A successful launch without the delusion of "balance" that so often leads to burnout, resentment, and failure.

Glass Priorities vs. Rubber Priorities

Not all priorities are created equal. Some things in your life are glass and will break if you drop them. Others are rubber and can survive being dropped, even a handful of times. The secret is knowing which is which in your current season of living.

Common Glass Priorities Right Now:

- Marriage during young kids phase
- Primary income during economic uncertainty
- Health maintenance during high-stress periods
- Being present during your kid's teenage years

Typical Rubber Priorities This Season:

- Social obligations that drain without bringing value
- Board positions that don't align with current priorities
- Important relationships that are in periods of low-need
- Entertainment habits that serve no larger purpose

You protect the glass. You let the rubber bounce.

The mistake most people make is treating rubber priorities like glass, and then wonder why critical things across your life are breaking. You can't bubble-wrap everything or you'll suffocate in the process. But distinguishing between glass and rubber isn't a one-time decision. Priorities shift between categories based on your season, your circumstances, and your long-term goals and priorities. What's a glass ball today might be rubber next month, and vice versa.

And when you focus on glass vs. rubber priorities and quit playing the balance game you'll quickly realize how much energy you were wasting on guilt. Think about it this way. You've got five gallons of energy every day. Right now, you're trying to pour a little bit into ten different buckets: your job, your kids, your health, your marriage, your side project, your parents, your friends, your house, your finances, your personal growth.

What do you get? Ten barely-wet buckets and a constant feeling like you're failing everywhere. And worse, you'll keep blaming yourself for not being "better at balance," when the problem was never your effort. It was your strategy. What if you poured those five gallons into the three buckets that actually matter this season? The other seven buckets? They can wait. Most of them don't even need water right now anyway.

But you won't do this because you're terrified of "disappointing" people. You'd rather disappoint yourself than have an awkward conversation with someone else about why you can't show up the way you're used to. The thing is, though, the people who matter will understand. The people who don't understand don't matter. And the buckets that actually need your attention right now will thank you for not half-assing them. Most of the pressure you're feeling to add water to non-critical buckets is self-imposed, and the people who would be impacted will be relieved when you have an honest conversation with them and create shared expectations. Realistic ones.

So stop spreading yourself thin because it feels noble. It's not noble. It's cowardly, because you're avoiding the hard choice of deciding what matters most.

Strategic No's vs. Reactive No's

Most people I coach operate from reactive no's. They're so overwhelmed or burned out that the no is coming while they're on the verge of hitting their breaking point. This creates a cycle where they overcommit, crash, kind of sort of recover... Then rinse and repeat. But strategic no's are different. They're decisions made from getting real about your current season in life, not from chaos about your current calendar.

A reactive no sounds like, "I can't take on anything else right now."

A strategic no sounds like, "That doesn't align with my priorities this quarter."

The difference is profound. Reactive no's come from weakness. Strategic no's come from strength. **When you're clear about your seasonal priorities (your vital few), saying no becomes an act of protecting what matters most, not avoiding what feels like too much to handle.**

I coach my clients to evaluate their commitments with these questions.

- Does this align with my current season's priorities?

- Am I saying yes from strategy or from obligation?
- If I say yes, what am I in turn saying no to?

This practice alone has saved countless clients from the scattered, high-activity but low-impact lifestyle that the "balance" lie creates.

Seasons Make Success Sustainable

The beauty of embracing seasons over balance is that it creates true sustainability. When you stop expecting yourself to advance everything simultaneously, you can go all-in where it matters most right now, knowing that other priorities will get their turn in future seasons. This creates a rhythm to life. Expansion and contraction. Intensity and recovery. And this prevents burnout while still allowing for extraordinary achievement.

A seasonal approach might look like this.

Quarter 1-2: Business growth season (primary) with relationship maintenance.

Quarter 3: Physical transformation season with business maintenance.

Quarter 4: Family depth season with fitness maintenance.

Year 2, Quarter 1: Relationship renewal with business innovation.

This approach is what prevented my client (earlier in the chapter) from crippling his business launch, by mistakenly attempting to be great in everything all at once. Instead, he could pour himself fully into one area while keeping the others healthy, knowing their time would come. And although some areas had progressed more than others, nothing had suffered. He'd honored the season each priority deserved instead of chasing all of them at once, realizing that every bucket didn't need water all the time. You have the power to negotiate with your buckets, and they'll appreciate you for it.

Stop Juggling Everything

You can't juggle three glass balls and twelve rubber, with nothing but your limited resources, and then be surprised when something crucial breaks. So what is your current "work-life balance" approach really costing you?

What's breaking while you're distracted by low priorities? The relationship that's dying from neglect. The health crisis building in the background. The kids who are learning that everyone gets your leftovers. The self-trust eroding every time you break another promise to yourself.

The way forward isn't to try harder at balancing. It's to stop trying to balance altogether. And then you need to sit down with pen and paper, and you need to make hard choices. What gets your five gallons this season and what you let run dry. Right now you make that call by reflex, handing your energy to whatever's loudest that morning. The overdue thing screaming in your inbox, or the squeakiest wheel (person) at your office.

Instead, choose through the lens of who you're becoming. Hold every option against the person on the other side of this season, the one you're actually building toward. What does he make room for? What does she protect when something has to give? Choose the sacrifice as that person, the same way you've been learning to since you stopped waiting to feel ready to move. That's the future you making the call, not the scared one from yesterday.

Cut from there and it lands differently. The sacrifice that felt like loss becomes alignment, because you're clearing space the person you're building truly needs.

So take a few minutes to think strategically.

- Name your season honestly
- Choose your vital few priorities
- Schedule when other priorities will get their turn (and let them know)
- Brainstorm what boundaries and process could protect those priorities
- Identify conversations needed to create shared expectations
- Reflect daily on how you're managing glass vs. rubber priorities

Clarity doesn't make hard choices easy, but it does eliminate the vague guilt that's been clouding your every decision. Every tradeoff reinforces your standards or erodes them. And over time, those standards shape the person you become.

Write down the tradeoff you've been pretending isn't happening. It could be the relationship with your partner while you chase the promotion at work. Then name exactly what it's costing you. Be specific. Be honest. Because the real cost isn't the tradeoff you're avoiding. It's the critical parts of your life you're destroying while you keep pretending you can have it all at once.

The Truth

Balance isn't something you achieve. It's something you chase while everything that actually matters gets a fraction of what's needed, and low priorities get way too much of your resources.

The people living the lives you want aren't balanced. They're focused. They've made hard choices about what this season demands, and they've stopped apologizing for what had to wait.

Tradeoffs are proof your life means something. Anything worth building costs something.

If this one hit hard: Chapter 15 (Your Real Values Show Up in Hard Choices) is where you find out what you actually value versus what you say you value. That gap lives in exactly these kinds of tradeoffs. Chapter 16 (You Can't Win the Game If You're Playing the Wrong Role) takes it one step further. This chapter decided where your energy goes. That one decides who you become when you get there.

MINI: You're Scrolling Your Life Away.

You spent more time researching your last Netflix binge than the content that's rewiring your brain. Then you wonder why you feel unfocused and constantly behind.

Your phone buzzes. Another opinion. Another reason to feel angry, envious, or distracted. You tell yourself you'll check for a minute, and twenty minutes later you surface foggy and irritated, wondering where the time went. You know exactly what's happening. You do it anyway. It's like complaining about being sick between bites of your third McDonald's combo of the day.

So yeah, be pissed. Just point it at the right person. Nobody force-fed you that feed. You built it, one follow at a time, and now it's feeding you back. Everything you consume is either growing weeds or growing fruit up there in your head. There's no neutral setting.

Follow accounts that make you feel like garbage, and congratulations, you're farming insecurity. Mainline outrage content all day and your brain gets very, very good at two things. Hunting for problems and then losing your mind over them. Whether they're real or not. Let in the hustle-bros who sell shortcuts, and you train yourself to expect everything to be fast, easy, and free. If it's not (and what in the world worth having is?) then you convince yourself it didn't matter anyways. But it totally did.

You think you're "just scrolling." You're actually running thousands of tiny training sessions, and your brain is sitting front row with pen and notebook, ready to soak it all up.

Then you sit across from people like me, frustrated because you can't stick to anything and wondering why you feel scattered and stuck. The answer is usually located right there on the table beside you, buzzing with another notification.

You can't become disciplined while consuming undisciplined content, or build self-reputation while following people who mock effort. You can't think long-term while feeding your brain short-term dopamine hits disguised as productivity.

We're told identity change comes from willpower or big life decisions. It doesn't. Your identity is being shaped by thousands of micro-inputs every single day. The podcasts in your earbuds during your commute. The accounts in your feed you scroll while waiting in line.

The fastest way to change who you are? Change what you tolerate in your social feeds and other media across your life. Unfollow the accounts that spin you up without offering any sort of real value. And please, for the love of all things holy, stop consuming content that makes you feel like your life isn't enough.

Choose books, podcasts, and conversations that challenge you to think bigger, not smaller. Because long before your identity shifts in public, it gets programmed by repetition. By the quiet content you let in when no one is around.

You're not just curating content. You're curating character. And if you don't control the feed, it will rewrite your future self without your permission. Because that future identity is being shaped right now, one scroll at a time. The only question is whether you're directing that process or letting it happen by accident.

MINIs are usually where I let you off the hook, but not this one. It's something that you MUST act on right now, if you ever want a chance at breaking this toxic cycle in your life.

CHALLENGE

For 24 hours, write down EVERYTHING you let into your mind. Every article, video, conversation, piece of content. Then ask yourself, does this consumption pattern belong to someone building the life I want? Or someone just trying to get through the day?

And don't stop at just one day. Make it a weekly ritual. Every Sunday night, run the reflection again. What voices dominated my mind this week? What content pulled me forward? What content pulled me down? What needs to go, and what needs more space?

Then edit ruthlessly. Your identity doesn't just shift in big moments... It also shifts while you're scrolling in line at Starbucks.

Chapter 10

Protocol Over Promises.

THE LIE: You know exactly what to do. The follow-through just has to wait until you feel motivated enough, or until life settles down. Consistency is a matter of catching the right state of mind.
WHY IT HOLDS: Because motivation does show up sometimes, and when it does the work feels almost effortless. What you don't see is that you're building your identity around the feeling, not the behavior. And feelings are the least reliable foundation you could choose.

A single belief is a brick. And a brick alone holds nothing.

Stack enough of them without anything binding them together, and you've built a wall that looks solid right up until the first real storm leans on it. Then it comes down. Every time. You're left wondering why you fall apart every time life leans on you, always picking up the pieces and never sure why.

That's what's happening. And it's fixable.

But Protocol is the mortar you've been missing. It's the thing that turns a pile of hopeful bricks into a solid wall that holds weight, takes a hit, and gets stronger for it. Everything you've learned so far was a brick. This chapter is where you learn to make the mortar.

The Protocol Reset

Self-trust works the same way. You can't think it into existence, manifest it, or borrow it from someone else's success story. It's earned, one piece of evidence at a time, by saying you'll do something and then doing it. Your Protocol is where that evidence comes from. It's your proof of who you are. Not who you want to be or who you could become. Who you actually are, right now, when it counts.

Jeff came to me after his third attempt at starting his own business had failed. Brilliant guy and full of great ideas. But every time he got close to launching, he'd find a reason to delay, pivot, or quit entirely.

"I don't understand it," he told me. "I know I can do this. I've got the skills. But every time I'm about to pull the trigger, I just... Don't."

Was he afraid of failure? Sure. But that wasn't the root issue. Neither was it his business plan or market conditions, although I humored him and reviewed them "just in case." The problem was Jeff had trained himself not to trust his own word. He'd wake up planning to work on his business for three hours, then spend that time reorganizing his office instead. He'd commit to reaching out to five potential clients, then find a million reasons why the timing wasn't right. He'd promise himself he'd finish his website by Friday, then move the deadline to next Friday. Then the Friday after that.

Every broken promise to himself was one more piece of evidence behind "I'm someone who doesn't follow through." And when you don't trust yourself to follow through on small commitments, why would you trust yourself with big ones?

So we designed Jeff a Protocol that was simple, but absolute.

Week One: Check business email at exactly 9AM and immediately respond to anything that could be handled in under five minutes.

Week Two: Add a 30-minute focused work block immediately after email, no exceptions. Bonus points for identifying targeted actions ahead of time.

Week Three: Add one client outreach action per day during that work block, in addition to any other key objectives.

Week Four: Add a Friday review of the week's progress and then map next week's priorities.

No motivation required. No inspiration needed. Just the Protocol.

The first week was harder than he expected. Jeff would forget, then remember at 10:30AM and feel tempted to skip the commitment entirely. But we had determined it was absolute, so he stuck to it. By week two, the 9AM email routine had become automatic. By week three, he was looking forward to that focused work block because he could feel his self-reputation growing, and he had really gotten into the silly "bonus points" activities we'd outlined. And most days he even found himself keeping the momentum going well beyond the initial time limit he had set for his work blocks.

A few months later, Jeff had launched his business and landed his first three clients. He'd rebuilt his identity one kept promise at a time. He'd proven to himself that when he says something will happen, it happens. That evidence became the foundation for bigger commitments, bolder actions, and, eventually, the business he'd been trying to build for years. Yes, there were tough weeks where a rough Monday would spin him out, and we'd have to get back to basics and reconnect with his foundational Protocol. But the goal is to not let one step backwards turn into a dozen. Failing is fine, and even expected. But fail forward. Take a breather, then reengage your Protocol from where you are, not where you wish you were.

Common Failure Patterns

Before you start building your own Protocol, let's address the potential elephant in the room... You've probably tried this before. Maybe not exactly this approach with this exact title. But you've set goals, made commitments, and tried to build habits.

And you failed.

What I see most often in my practice are these patterns.

The Perfectionist sets a morning routine with several components, executes it flawlessly for a few days before oversleeping on the fourth. Then, instead of even attempting just one action from their list, they declare the whole system broken and drop it entirely. Their identity shifts from "I'm building consistency" to "I can't do anything right."

The Overbuilder decides to transform their entire life all at once. They commit to working out daily, eating clean, journaling, meditating, and reading for thirty minutes. The first day or two feels great. It's tough, but they're hanging in there. But by week two, they're missing workouts and their books have begun collecting dust. Week three, they're eating pizza and beating themselves up about it. Their identity shifts from "I'm changing my life" to "Change is too complicated anyways."

The Restarter breaks their streak and immediately begins planning their next great attempt, set to begin the following Monday. Because Monday is logical.

They've started the same "life change" cycle eight times this year, each time with renewed enthusiasm and slightly updated plans. Their identity shifts from "I'm someone learning to follow through" to "I'm someone who never finishes anything."

Notice the patterns? None of them were lacking in willpower or motivation. Some of them had inspiration in spades. They were willing to put the work into building and attempting a new system. Yet once their focus shifted to perfection or to massive scale, they fell apart. But Protocol is about persistence through imperfection. Because you will, inevitably, break your Protocol. Just like all three of these examples did. We all do. But what matters most is what happens next, how you respond to the misstep. Skim the patterns above again and identify the key break points.

Missing once is data. Something disrupted your system. Maybe you traveled, got sick, or had a crisis. This is information. Ask yourself, what changed? How can I account for this variable next time?

Missing twice is danger. Now you're creeping into pattern territory. Your brain starts building the story that this protocol "doesn't work" or that you're "not consistent." For most, though, this is the moment that determines whether you build long-term self-trust or erode it further.

Missing three times is a new identity forming. You're no longer someone who does this thing. You're someone who used to do this thing. Your Protocol isn't broken. It never was. But your belief in your ability to execute is.

The repair isn't complicated, but it requires you to abandon the perfectionist mindset that kills most transformation attempts.

Step 1: Acknowledge without drama. "I broke my Protocol. This is data, not evidence of poor character."

Step 2: Recommit, don't restart. You don't need a new protocol or a new start date. You need to do the thing today, right now, regardless of what has happened up to this point.

Step 3: Adjust for reality. If your Protocol was broken by predictable life circumstances, consider modifying it. The goal isn't to maintain the same routine across all possible conditions, but to maintain the identity of someone who keeps commitments to themselves regardless of circumstances.

Your Protocol serves your identity, not the other way around. A flexible protocol that you can maintain builds more self-trust than a rigid one that breaks under pressure.

Last, account for your surroundings. The most successful protocols are powered in part by environmental design, since your physical space either supports or sabotages your Protocol.

Make it inevitable. If your Protocol is to read for fifteen minutes when you wake up, put the book on your pillow the night before. If it's to do pushups after you get out of bed, clear a space on your bedroom floor. Remove every possible barrier between intention and action.

Make alternatives harder. If your Protocol is to check your priorities before checking your phone, plug your phone in across the room. If it's to drink water first thing in the morning, put a glass beside your bed and leave your coffee maker unplugged.

Create visual cues. Your environment should remind you of who you're becoming. The book beside your toothbrush is proof you prioritize learning. The workout clothes laid out the night before are evidence you move your body.

This is about creating an environment that puts your Protocol onto the path of least resistance. When your space supports your Protocol, you're not fighting yourself every day. You're working with your psychology and not against it.

The Identity Engine in Motion

Your Protocol is meant to feed your Identity Engine good, clean fuel. You're someone who honors your word regardless of your feelings and that your self-reputation matters. After all, the action could be anything.

- Reading for 15 minutes before checking your phone
- Writing three sentences in a journal every night
- Doing ten pushups when you get out of bed
- Reviewing your calendar every Sunday at 6PM
- Making one new, meaningful professional connection per week

What matters isn't what you choose. What matters is that you choose something specific, commit to it completely, and execute it consistently. Each time you follow through, you stack proof behind "I'm someone who does what I say I'll do." Each time you don't, you stack proof for the opposite. This is Protocol + the Identity Engine in full practice. Your Engine isn't powered by vision boards, mantras, or hits of inspiration. It's powered by Protocol. By small promises kept with relentless consistency. By a system of action that makes your future identity inevitable, not optional.

The Identity Engine has three moving parts.

Your Protocol. The actions you repeat, regardless of how you feel.

Your Self-Reputation. That's the recorded ledger from Chapter 3, the evidence your actions build about who you really are. Your Protocol is the depositing system. Every rep you didn't feel like doing and did anyway posts to the record, and the record is the only thing your subconscious actually believes.

Your Core Beliefs. The identity you begin to trust because it's grounded in proof, not hope.

This is how identity actually shifts through the Identity Engine in motion.

Action → Evidence → Identity → More Aligned Action

That's the behavior loop from the introduction, drawn as a system you can actually run and one that focuses on identity change. And that loop is always running. The only question is whether it's fueled by the Protocol you chose or driven by the defaults you didn't.

What's this look like in action? Weeks one through two, your Protocol feels mechanical and forced. Weeks three through four, it finally starts to feel natural and you'll notice when you haven't done it. By month two, it's become part of who you are. You've begun to see yourself as someone who follows through. Months three and beyond, you'll find yourself naturally making and keeping bigger commitments because you trust yourself to follow through on what you're perceiving as higher stakes.

Your Protocol, Your Choice

The most successful people I work with all have non-negotiables. Their goals are almost all different, and their ambitions are all over the place. But they all possess a handful of core non-negotiables. These are the behaviors they do regardless of circumstances or feelings.

One CEO I coach has three non-negotiables:

- Review the previous day's decisions every morning before checking email, text, or social media.
- Walk for 20 minutes after lunch, without devices.
- End each day by reviewing tomorrow's calendar and identifying its priorities.

It doesn't matter if he's traveling, sick, or dealing with a crisis. These three things happen. Because they're about who he is at his core, not simple gestures at productivity.

An entrepreneur I work with has different non-negotiables:

- Read one article about her industry every day.
- Send one message to someone in her network.
- Transfer some amount of money to her business savings, even if it's just $5.

When she first identified these non-negotiables, her business was struggling and her confidence was shot. But those three simple protocols gave her something she could control when everything else felt chaotic. It took just over a year, but those habits compounded into industry expertise, a strong professional network, and the financial discipline that funded her business growth. Keeping those habits proved she was someone who could be trusted with bigger challenges.

I have my own set of non-negotiables. Two core ones that never change, and I typically rotate another one or two depending on my season of life. The two, though?

- Plan tomorrow today. I never end a workday without knowing what tomorrow's "good day" looks like, so I can wake up and push play.
- Plan my fun, and earn it. Nobody can work nonstop, so I block two or three recharge windows across the day. Each one gets earned by finishing the work in front of it.

Yours will look different, and they should. Borrow some of these if you just need to get going, but non-negotiables should be tuned to your goals, your context, and your season of life.

Designing your Protocol starts with five rules.

Start impossibly small. Choose something so easy you can't rationalize your way out of it. If you're thinking "that's too simple," you're probably on the right track.

Make it binary. Either you did it or you didn't. No partial credit, no "close enough." Binary outcomes build the most unmistakable evidence.

Remove variables. Same time, same place, same methodology. The fewer decisions required, the more likely you are to follow through when your motivation is low.

Track the streak. Not for public affirmation, but for you. Your brain needs to see the evidence accumulating.

Protect it like your reputation depends on it. Because it does. Every time you're tempted to skip it, remember that this isn't just about the action itself. This is about building self-reputation.

And three changes will happen once your Protocol is up and consistently running. Think of these like big dominos in your life that, once tipped, make all the other dominos more likely to fall as well.

Decision fatigue disappears. You stop asking "Should I?" and start operating from "I do." There's no mental negotiation, as you've automated the behavior that proves your identity.

Confidence becomes internalized. Instead of needing to convince yourself you're capable, you have daily evidence. Your confidence stops being loud and aspirational, and it becomes steady and earned.

Setbacks become temporary. When life disrupts your routine, you don't spiral into an existential crisis. And life will exert force on your Protocol every single day. But you have a track record of consistency to fall back on. Bad days don't define you because you have undeniable evidence of who you are when you're working your Protocol.

This is the compound effect of consistency. You have internalized the truth that you're someone who can be trusted with bigger challenges and ambitious goals. That's the real power of your Protocol. It's not about the fifteen minutes of reading or the ten pushups or the daily email check. It's about proving to yourself that your word holds value. First for yourself, and then for the world.

Protocol becomes reputation. Reputation becomes belief. Belief powers bigger action.

CHALLENGE

Right now, choose one micro-commitment. Something you can do every day for the next seven days without fail.

Make it:

- **Specific** (exactly what, when, where)
- **Binary** (you either did it or you didn't)
- **Ridiculously small** (30 seconds to 5 minutes maximum)

Write it down: "For the next 7 days, I will _______ at _______ every day."

Then do it. Don't wait until you feel ready. Don't tell yourself you'll start Monday. You've made those promises before, and you're here reading a book literally called *Stop Lying to Yourself*.

Start today and prove that this time is different... Because you are.

The Truth

Your brain doesn't believe your intentions. It believes your track record. And right now, that track record is telling a story you probably don't love.

You don't rebuild self-trust with grand gestures or fresh starts. You rebuild it with small promises kept quietly, repeatedly, when nobody's watching and nothing's forcing you.

Protocol becomes reputation. Reputation becomes belief. Belief powers bigger action. That's how life and progress actually work.

If this one hit hard: Chapter 13 (Borrowed Identity Always Breaks) gets into what happens when the systems you're running aren't actually yours. Chapter 18 (The Work Evolves. It Never Ends.) is the honest truth about what Protocol looks like over the long haul, after the early momentum is gone and it's just you and the commitments you made.

PART 2: IDENTITY RECONSTRUCTION

MINI: 5-Star Personal Brand. 1-Star Character.

You can have a resume that makes people jealous while having a relationship with yourself that makes you ashamed.

Let's be real. Resumes are theater. LinkedIn profiles have become works of fiction more creative than anything Netflix has ever produced. "Results-oriented leader with a passion for synergistic solutions." Translation: you survived three reorganizations without getting fired. Your bio mentions you "spearheaded transformational initiatives" when you really just sent a lot of emails and hoped something would stick. You've got awards for "excellence" in categories so vague they could apply to anyone who showed up on time and kept their mouth shut.

Tragically, you put serious time and energy into crafting that depiction of yourself. You agonized over the wording. You A/B tested your LinkedIn headline like it was the most important project of the quarter. Meanwhile, the version of you that only you have access to... That one didn't get a single edit.

Behind the glossy headshots and buzzword bingo, you know what's actually true. You know about the promises you've broken to yourself. The standards you've quietly lowered when no one was watching. The conversations you've been dodging. The potential you've been hoarding as if it'll appreciate all on its own.

Your resume gets you job interviews. Your self-reputation determines whether you can sleep at night.

The world only sees your outcomes, but you have to live with your Protocol. Everyone sees the promotion... But only you know how many corners you cut to get it. Friends and followers see the "perfect" family photos... But only you know the number of meaningful conversations you've been avoiding. You either trust yourself or you don't. And trust, like muscle, is only built under tension.

Most people chase applause because they're terrified of the quiet. They're addicts who need a standing ovation just to feel like they exist. But the quiet is where it all actually happens. That's where you either do the thing you said you would, or you run a full mental gymnastics routine to explain why today is a perfectly justifiable exception. And those exceptions aren't harmless. They compound.

Do it enough times and you stop trusting yourself altogether. Not in a dramatic, rock-bottom kind of way. In the quiet, erosive way where you just stop making promises to yourself, because some part of you already knows you won't follow through.

Now look at what you've been protecting instead. Credentials, network, talent, all of that external stuff is fragile. Markets crash. Companies fold and whole industries routinely get disrupted. People forget your name faster than you'd like to believe.

But your relationship with yourself? That's your permanent roommate. And right now, a lot of you are living with someone you wouldn't trust to water your plants.

So what do you do with that? You stop performing for the audience. You stop announcing what you're going to do. You start stacking wins that nobody sees but you. And you let those wins be the evidence that rebuilds trust from the inside out. Not affirmations or agonized-over LinkedIn posts. Evidence. The kind that comes from actually doing what you said you'd do. Even when it's inconvenient or when "tomorrow" is sitting right there looking very freaking reasonable.

Some of you reading this are well-respected by everyone around you, but you don't respect yourself. You've mastered the external game while completely neglecting the internal one. You're like a luxury car with a broken engine. Impressive from the outside, but it won't even get you to the local grocery store.

What if you flipped it? What if your self-reputation became the only scoreboard that mattered? Not likes. Not titles. Not the performance of being "so busy" or "completely exhausted." Just one score... Did I keep my promises to myself today? Did I execute my Protocol?

When that's the metric, everything gets simpler. You stop chasing credibility and start building character. You stop needing validation and start stacking wins that only you know about, but wins that mean more than any post you've offered up to the LinkedIn gods.

That's where the real power lives. In knowing, deep down, that you don't need the world's approval. Because you've already earned your own.

Forget the resume theater and focus on your self-reputation. And if you don't like how it reads today, rewrite it tomorrow. But this time, don't use carefully considered words. Use actions.

Because your self-reputation isn't just about you. It's the energy your kids absorb. It's the standards your teammates inherit. It's the legacy you're writing whether you're paying attention to it or not.

Chapter II

You've Burned It Down. Now What?

WHAT YOU'RE BUILDING: Part 1 tore down the lies. Now you build. And the thing no one in the self-help aisle will admit is that when the old self came down, there was no special self waiting to be discovered. There's only the one you build from here. It's messy, and there'll never be a finish line you can see and sprint towards. But the self-trust and the beliefs you'll fail your way into... Those are the realest things you'll ever possess.

What you just did in Part 1, most people spend their entire lives avoiding. You've stopped lying to yourself about who you are, why you're stuck and what it's going to take to change. You've looked in the mirror and seen the truth. The actual YOU underneath all the excuses and inherited stories, not the one performed for others.

That took guts. Real fucking courage, not the motivational poster kind. And serious kudos to you.

So let's review everything you've accomplished, because you need to understand the ground you've covered before we talk about what comes next.

You confronted the uncomfortable reality that you've settled for comfort with a better view instead of actual transformation. You learned that your perspective isn't just a lens, but the architect of your reality, shaping what feels possible before you even try.

You discovered Promise Debt, the accumulated damage from every commitment you've broken to yourself. And you started clearing that debt through micro-promises that prove your word still means something.

Then you stopped waiting for someone else to rescue you and grabbed the wheel of your own life. From there, the Identity Engine took over, running on process instead of motivation. And you learned you can't skip the Desert because that's where real transformation happens.

You rebuilt confidence through evidence instead of affirmations, started living your montage instead of waiting for someone to film it, chose action over excuses, and stopped chasing the lie of balance.

If you've actually done this work (not just read about it, but lived it) you're probably feeling raw right now. Anyone would. You've torn down the structures that used to define you, and the space they left behind feels uncomfortably empty and exposed.

Which brings us to the question you're asking right now.

So what do I now build instead?

Part 1 was the deconstruction, the very necessary demolition of everything that couldn't hold your future. But deconstruction isn't the whole transformation. It's just the first step in a two-part process.

Many will get stuck at exactly this point. They've done the hard work of tearing down their old identity and confronting their lies. They feel different, even lighter in some ways... But now also unmoored. And that uncertainty makes them vulnerable to three massive mistakes that will waste everything they've accomplished thus far.

Mistake #1: They try to skip straight to tactics.

They want the morning routine. The productivity system. The exact steps to follow. "Just tell me what to do and I'll do it." But tactics without foundation are just new ways to perform the same old identity. You can follow someone else's morning routine perfectly and still end up exactly where you began, all because you never did the internal work to maintain any progress you might experience. Your performance will always regress to the underlying identity. Always.

I see this constantly with clients who've done the work to deconstruct a limiting identity, then immediately ask for a checklist to make tomorrow great. But tearing the old identity down and building the new one are two different jobs, and finishing the first doesn't mean you've touched the second. You get the first bits of evidence that a new identity is taking shape, and you decide you're ready to chase the "doing" of life. But abandon the new identity half-built, and the old one is still the strongest thing in you. It pulls you right back, and every tactic you were so eager to start comes down with it.

And, look. I get it. Identity work doesn't generate the instant gratification that the sexy 5AM routine you saw on Pinterest does. Replacing a limiting belief with an empowering one doesn't give you the shock and immediate sense of accomplishment that three minutes of a cold shower will. But I can promise you it'll generate mountains of greater fulfillment than a little cold water ever will.

Mistake #2: They retreat back to what's familiar.

The discomfort of not having a guarantee that they'll succeed in growing into their new identity starts to feel worse than the pain of being who they were. Or they question the payoff will be worth all of the pain. At least the old self was predictable. At least they knew how to navigate that identity, even if it wasn't working. So they rebuild the same structures they just demolished, maybe with slightly different paint. New goals, same old mindset. New habits, same old beliefs.

They mistake familiarity for direction and convince themselves that "Maybe it wasn't that bad after all." That the problem wasn't their identity, just their execution. It's okay for them to go back to who they were, and they'll just try harder this time. But there's no way in hell that's possible for you at this point. **You've seen too much and know too much. Going back is a slow death disguised as safety.**

Mistake #3: They wait for clarity before building.

As we discussed in Chapter 8, this is the most insidious trap because it feels like wisdom. They think transformation should come with a moment of cosmic revelation, the proverbial lightning bolt of insight that shows them exactly who they're supposed to become. So they keep searching and analyzing. They consume even more content, hoping the next book or course or guru will finally give them the answer they're desperately searching for.

"I just need to figure out my purpose first."

"I'm not ready to start building until I'm for sure about my next few steps."

But clarity doesn't come before building. It comes through building.

You don't figure out who you are and then become them. You become them and then figure out who you are.

You don't need more information. You've read enough, consumed enough, thought enough. You don't need another framework to study or another expert to follow. You don't need someone to tell you who you should become.

You need to start building. Flawed efforts. Imperfect designs. You need to be committed to building without knowing exactly how it will turn out. Because the person you're capable of becoming doesn't exist yet. And they're not buried inside waiting to be discovered. They're a blueprint you have to design and then construct, one choice at a time.

But that person will never exist if you keep waiting for permission (whether internal or external) to start.

From Archaeology to Architecture

You've spent Part 1 doing archaeological work. You've been digging through the layers of who you've been to this point, brushing off the lies and examining what's been buried. That work was necessary. You needed to understand what you've been carrying that was never yours to begin with.

You excavated your Promise Debt and discovered the cost of broken commitments, and you've found the stories you've been telling yourself about why change is hard, why you're stuck, why you can't have what you want. But now the work changes completely. You're no longer an archaeologist searching for some "true self" buried under years of conditioning. You're an architect designing the blueprint for who you're becoming.

Archaeologists and architects might both work with structures, but they operate from completely different paradigms. And to be clear, there's nothing wrong with archaeology. Therapy can feel like archaeology, and good therapy changes lives. Understanding the site you're standing on, what was buried there, who buried it... That's real work, and you did a form of it through all of Part 1. But archaeology's job is to understand the ground. It was never going to build the house.

Archaeologists dig backward. They're searching for something preexisting, something waiting to be found. It's facing rearward, with an emphasis on interacting with the past. So it's dependent on what's already there.

Architects start with a vision and create something that doesn't exist yet. They draft plans, test them against reality, redesign when the structure doesn't hold, and keep building until they've constructed something that can carry the weight it's meant to bear. Their work is active. It's intentional. It's creative.

Most people treat personal development like archaeology. They think their job is to dig deep enough, search long enough, try enough frameworks until they finally uncover their "authentic self", that perfect version of them that's been waiting to be discovered all along.

But that's not how identity works. Your authentic self isn't hiding. It's not buried. It doesn't even exist yet. Who you're capable of becoming is something you have to intentionally design and systematically build through decisions that either prove or disprove the identity you're trying to construct.

After Part 1, you might be tempted to keep digging, hoping to prove me wrong and find that ideal self that's supposedly waiting to be discovered underneath all the layers. But, please trust me, you've already done that work. The site is excavated and the rubble of broken promises has been removed. (At least, if you really did the work from each chapter...)

<u>The ground is clear. Now you have to build.</u>

Building means making decisions with incomplete information. It means testing beliefs you've chosen instead of blindly living by ones you inherited. It means failing at new attempts and treating those failures as data, not verdicts on your worth or capability. Through keeping promises when it's the last thing you *feel* like doing, and behaving like the person you're becoming even before you *feel* like that person.

The blueprint you're about to design won't be perfect on the first draft. Your early attempts at building will expose flaws you couldn't see in the planning phase. You'll make mistakes that force you to redesign sections you thought were solid. But that's not failure. That's construction. Every building project has setbacks. Materials don't perform as expected. Weather delays progress. Structural issues emerge during execution that weren't visible in the blueprint. Architects don't abandon the project when this happens, though. They adapt, redesign, and then they keep building.

That's what Part 2 is about. Not finding yourself, but building yourself. Not digging for someone who was already there, but constructing someone new through progressive failure, one tested decision at a time.

The Frameworks Ahead

Over the next several chapters, you're going to learn how identity gets built when you stop searching and start constructing. The practice, not the theory. What works when life tests you, not what sounds inspiring on TikTok. You'll learn that identity is built through progressive failure, not perfect execution. Your first plan is supposed to break. That's not evidence you're doing it wrong, that's how you gather the data to build a stronger way forward. The old pattern says quit when the initial blueprint fails. You're going to learn to treat that failure as essential feedback, not final judgment.

Borrowed identity always breaks under pressure. The confident person you're pretending to be will crumble the moment life punches you in the mouth with a high-stakes situation. But the identity you've earned through evidence, through doing the hard things when no one's watching? That's unshakeable. You can't rent character. You have to build it.

Beliefs are the invisible architecture determining what you think is possible. Most of what you currently believe, you never chose. Those beliefs were inherited from parents who were scared, teachers who played it safe, and a culture that confused humility with invisibility. Part 2 is about designing and living into the beliefs that will support the life you want to build instead of the one you've been conditioned to accept.

Your real values aren't the ones you post on LinkedIn or write on vision boards. They're the ones that show up when you're forced to choose between two things you want, when keeping one means sacrificing the other. Hard choices don't just reveal who you are, they also construct who you're becoming.

You're playing different roles across your life, and much of your struggle comes from bringing the wrong energy to the wrong moment. The executive who runs dinner like a board meeting isn't being effective, they're being inappropriate. Context determines which role needs to show up.

And you're exhausted from years of keeping a house show-ready for potential buyers you'll never get to know, much less care about. It's exhausting in a way that feels soul-deep. The disconnection and the feelings that nothing matters? That's not some buried true self clawing to get out. It's the exhaustion of maintaining a performance you no longer believe in, and the pull to finally put it down.

These are the sequential building blocks behind intentional identity (re)construction. Each one builds on what came before, and each prepares you for what's coming next. Together, they form the architecture of transformation, the systematic process of becoming someone who can hold what you're trying to build.

Part 1 cleared the ground and showed you what needed to be demolished. Part 2 shows you how to build on the foundation you created in that process.

Your Choice

This next section of the book will ask something different of you than Part 1 did.

Part 1 required honesty. The courage to look at yourself without flinching or making excuses. The willingness to admit you've been lying to yourself about who you are, why you're stuck, and what it's going to take to change.

Part 2 requires action. Reading alone won't do it. You have to actively build, applying the frameworks to your real life even when it's uncomfortable. Yes, at times it'll suck.

You can read every word of the next several chapters and still change nothing. Nod along with every framework, relate to every story, appreciate every insight, and still stay exactly who you are right now. The chapters will make sense. The examples will resonate. You might even take notes, highlight passages, tell yourself you're going to implement what you're learning. But unless you treat these frameworks as construction plans, as blueprints you'll use to build something real, nothing will change. You'll close this book feeling inspired... But unchanged. Informed but not transformed.

Or you can commit to the harder thing.

You can get to building. You can test these frameworks in your real life with your real problems and your very real resistance. You can use progressive failure to design an identity that works for you instead of copying someone else's fiction. You can choose beliefs that serve your future instead of defending ones that protected your past.

And it's going to be really fucking uncomfortable. I would never sugarcoat that truth. It's going to require you to act before you feel ready, to build before you know what the final product will even look like, and to become someone new while still feeling like the old you.

But the person you were when you started this book is already gone. And the gap between who you are and who you're capable of being has a face now, and your Promise Debt has a number.

The ground is cleared. You know what needed to be demolished, and you've done the archaeological work of understanding what you've been carrying.

Now it's time to build.

Stop Lying. Start Building.

The ground has been cleared.

And now you're sitting with the question Chapter 11 leaves you holding... What do you build next? Not theoretically. Not someday. Right now, with the real discomfort and resistance, and the very real possibility that you'll retreat to familiar territory the moment life turns the difficulty level up to 10. Which it will, you know this.

The book will take you through it. Everything you need to build is in Part 2.

But some of you already know your own pattern here. You love learning new frameworks. Following through (consistently, without structure, without someone holding you to it) is where you've always come apart.

"Stop Lying. Start Building." is the implementation course built around Part 2. A structured, accountable path through the construction, with someone who's logged 9,000+ hours of 1:1 coaching in exactly this work.

You cleared the ground. What goes up next is a choice. Make it on purpose, with my direct support or not. But on purpose.

MINI: The Dream Showed Up. You Weren't Ready.

Everyone's got their lottery fantasy.

Private jet to Bali. Mansion with a pool shaped like your middle finger. Walking into your boss's office and telling them exactly what you think of their "urgent" emails about cover sheets on TPS reports.

Sweet revenge served with a huge side of financial freedom.

Unfortunately, lots of people will achieve their dream or big, audacious goal before they've become someone who can handle the weight of that new reality.

Sorry to ruin your daydream, but (according to many outlets) nearly one-third of lottery winners declare bankruptcy within 3-5 years. *Record scratch... Plot twist.* It turns out getting rich quick and staying rich are entirely different skill sets. Shocker, I know.

Take Jack Whittaker, who won $314.9 million in the Powerball at 55, when he already had $17 million from his construction business. This wasn't some naive kid. This was a successful businessman who had an identity that could handle a few million dollars. But not one that could handle hundreds of millions of dollars.

Within a year, he was carrying around $500,000 in cash in a briefcase and getting robbed at strip clubs. By 2007, he was saying "I wish I'd torn that ticket up." By the time he died, he was believed to be broke.

Other reporting finds 44% of lottery winners have spent all of their winnings within five years. Not bankrupt, but back to their default identity. And bank balance. Five years! That's faster than most people change their phone cases.

The thing nobody mentions in those "manifest your millions" Instagram posts? **Your bank account can write checks that your character can't cash.**

Success isn't just an achievement you unlock like some video game trophy. It's weight you carry. And if you haven't been to the gym (metaphorically speaking) it's going to flatten you faster than a steamroller on espresso. The dream business that becomes a nightmare because you behaved as if "visionary leader" and "chaos creator" were the same job description. The relationship that implodes because you confused having standards with having opinions about everything.

Most people think they're waiting on their big break. They've got it backwards. The break was never the hard part. Plenty of people get it and lose it inside a year. What you're actually waiting on is you, on becoming someone who can still be holding the thing a year after it lands.

Because those lottery winners had to learn this life lesson the hard way, and everyone chasing external success needs to understand it, too. Who you become determines what you can hold. This is physics with feelings, not a cheap mantra.

You can't run enterprise software on a calculator and expect it not to crash. Just like you can't handle a ten-pound dream with two-pound habits and wonder why everything keeps falling apart.

The version of you that gets the dream and the one that keeps the dream? They might share a name, but they're boxers in different weight classes. Becoming successful requires hunger and hustle and maybe even some strategic luck. But keeping it requires becoming someone who naturally operates at that level, not someone visiting success like a tourist. You must become someone who actually lives there.

Want to hold more? Build the frame first.

Champion-level behaviors aren't complicated. They're just consistent. Say no without needing to explain or apologize. Choose long-term alignment over short-term gratification. Turn failure into feedback without spiraling into self-pity. Don't chase validation, and instead focus on attracting respect through competence.

You want a big life? Then train like you'll have to carry double its weight. If you're not there yet, then you've found your training program. You don't need the dream yet. You need the reps. You need to build into the YOU that the dream requires.

Because when you become that person, really become them and not just play dress-up for the interview, the dream doesn't just arrive. It sticks around instead of ghosting you like a bad Tinder date.

Chapter 12

This Is Where You Always Quit.

WHAT YOU'RE BUILDING: The construction method itself. Your first blueprint is going to break, probably even within the week. But the break is the point. Every failed attempt hands you data the planning phase never could. The deposits that rebuild a bankrupt self-reputation only count in the stretch where quitting feels reasonable. Which is exactly where you've always quit before.

As you begin building forward, you have to fully embrace your new role of architect and let the archaeology work go. And as you do, remember that architects never get it "right" on the first blueprint. So screwups don't equal failure. Think of them as stress tests on a system you haven't finished building yet.

A couple of months ago, you finally got serious about change. You mapped out the new morning routine and bought all the "right" books. You cleared your calendar of the distractions that had been quietly sabotaging your progress for months. You even told a few people about your commitment. Partly for accountability, partly because you were excited about who you were attempting to become.

And for a week, maybe even two, it worked. You felt different. You even started to think, *this time is actually different.*

Then life handed you a really freaking rough day and your system fell apart. All good, you'll get back on the horse tomorrow. But, for the most part, you don't. You sleep in a bit and miss your gym time, and you spend the morning doomscrolling before even getting up to brush your teeth. And the routine that felt so natural during week one suddenly felt forced. Unrealistic. And all of your old patterns didn't just creep back in, they kicked the fucking door wide open.

And that's when the old inner voice showed up. The one that whispers, "See? Same old you. You're not meant for this."

But that's bullshit. You're fully capable of pulling this off. You failed because you're building something new, and building (real building) is messy, iterative, and full of stress tests that expose exactly what needs to be reinforced. **Most people treat failure like a judgment when it's nothing more than a dataset.** And a critical one.

Your First Plan Is Supposed to Break

Like I mentioned last chapter, there's a meaningful difference between archaeologists and architects. Archaeologists work backward, hoping to uncover something preexisting and just waiting to be discovered. It's a role that had its place in your growth journey. Architects iterate forward. They start with a vision, draft a blueprint, and then test it against reality. When the structure wobbles (and it will wobble), they don't abandon the project. They go back to the drawing board. They strengthen what's weak. They redesign what didn't hold, and then they build again.

And that process looks nothing like a straight line. It looks like Progressive Failure... Intentional experimentation that brings you closer to something that works, one broken attempt at a time. It's not pretty when it's happening, but it's the only identity building process that works. When a client comes to me devastated because their "perfect plan" fell apart, I usually find myself sitting in extended silence while they vent. They sit across from me, frustrated and convinced they've just proven they're not cut out for the change they want. They recite their failures like evidence in a case against themselves. "I lasted two weeks with the morning routine." "I made it three days with the boundary I set." "I wrote for a week and then stopped."

I wait out their rant until a very long, uncomfortable silence stretches, and then ask them, "What did you learn?"

"What do you mean?"

"What did the failures teach you about how you truly operate? What did breaking the plan reveal about what needs to be adjusted?"

Nine times out of ten, they look at me like I'm speaking a foreign language. And that's because they were taught to see failure as a final grade instead of a rough draft.

But your first attempt at any meaningful change is never supposed to work perfectly. It's supposed to show you what doesn't work so you can build something that does. That morning routine that crumbled? It wasn't designed for your actual life, it was designed for the idealized version of your life that exists only in your head when you're feeling motivated. Now you have data about the gap between that fantasy and what's reality. That's intelligence, not failure.

That boundary you set that felt awkward and got tested immediately? You learned something about how people respond when you start changing the rules of engagement on them. And in doing so, you learned something about your own discomfort with potentially disappointing others. That's evidence that you're finally pressing against the limits of who you've been up to this point in your life, not a sign of weakness.

Your first plan is supposed to break so that you can now build a better one.

Progressive Failure Is the System

Progressive Failure is the practice of testing your mindsets and systems under real-world conditions, collecting feedback from what works and what doesn't, and then using that feedback to build something stronger. It's not random failure. It's not hoping things work out. It's the intentional stress-testing of your new identity, with the understanding that what survives the test is what you get to keep. It's tempting to avoid this process because it doesn't feel like growth. In the moment, it feels like a setback. A big one. It feels like evidence that you're not disciplined enough, or committed enough, or even strong enough to change. That's because we've been conditioned to believe transformation should feel smooth and inspirational, like that classic 3-minute movie montage where everything falls into place (instead of the real 3-month slog that took place within the film's story).

But real-life transformation feels more like controlled demolition. You're tearing down the parts of your old system that can't support your new life, and you're building new structures that can. That process is supposed to be uncomfortable. It's supposed to expose where you're weak, where you're unprepared and need more support. The discomfort isn't a bug. It's a critical feature telling you where to keep pushing your resources.

I've watched the same change patterns surface over and over within my clients. And they're worth naming, because there's a solid chance you'll recognize yourself in at least one of them.

The first pattern is the person who designs a flawless plan and then abandons it the moment *anything* goes wrong. Not when everything goes wrong, but when *anything* goes wrong. One crack and they declare the whole structure unsound. They treat imperfection as failure, which means they never build anything because nothing survives contact with real life without a crack or two. They're not afraid of failure, exactly. They're afraid of what failure might confirm about them. So they quit before the evidence becomes anything resembling conclusive.

The second pattern is the person who tries something, it doesn't work, and they immediately try something completely different. Whole new system with different frameworks. As if the problem was the plan and not the behavioral patterns they brought to it. What they keep skipping is the most important step in the whole process... Reflection. They never sit long enough with what broke to understand *why* it broke. So they carry the same blind spots from one attempt to the next, just dressed up in different language.

Then there's the third type. It's much more rare than the first two, but a real one. This is the person who actually does the thing. They design, test, fail, extract the lesson, adjust, and go again. They're willing to be uncomfortable long enough to collect the data needed to keep redesigning their way forward. This has nothing to do with willpower or even discipline. You can still be disciplined in your pursuit of all the wrong behavioral patterns. These people have just stopped treating failure like a verdict and started treating it like information.

Most people spend their lives rotating between the first two. But your goal is to become the third type.

The Data Extraction Process

I rebuilt my coaching brand identity six times in my first four years of striking out on my own. Each iteration taught me something the previous one couldn't possibly access. And while any single "failure" would have been enough to break down the thousands of people who attempt to become life coaches each year, I clung to being that third type of person. Sometimes desperately. And these failures cost me tens of thousands of dollars in sunk marketing costs and hundreds of hours in building products almost no one purchased. But I am where I am today (waiting list, coaching fees that I determine and don't negotiate) because I used each failure to learn 1-2 critical lessons to inform the next level of my practice. If you're wondering why I never quit, I'd love to tell you I was fearless or something cool like that. I wasn't. I just decided, early and stubbornly, that quitting cost more than failing.

That time I was going to become the next viral online coach with the huge library of online courses? Tens of thousands of dollars and hundreds of hours for a single sale of $97. Any "reasonable" human would call that an abject failure and wonder how long it took me to head back to corporate America. I called it expensive education about what I'm good at and where I still needed to grow.

The parent coaching brand? Every test group raved. Market research suggested I'd captured the next big thing. Five months and thousands in ad spend later? Complete flop. Turns out, parents don't want to pay hundreds or even thousands of dollars to admit they need help in what is probably the most intimate relationship any of us will ever have. That "failure" taught me more about market psychology than any success could have... And how much to trust "market research experts."

But to extract value from failure, you have to sit in it. You have to dissect it and pick apart every decision made along the way, big or small, and find the lessons hiding in the wreckage. The standard responses are denying the failure or drowning in it, and neither one works. Every failure I've experienced has refined who I'm becoming and what I'm building. Take this book. It NEVER would have existed without all of my previous brand failures. Every single one of them taught me lessons that have been distilled into these pages, that kept refining the frameworks that I'm now sharing with you. But no matter how much shame or even physical nausea I might have felt, I had to really dig my hands into each of those experiences.

There's a five-step process I use with clients to turn failure into fuel.

Step 1: Pause Before You Pivot. When something breaks, resist the urge to immediately try something different. Sit with the failure for at least 24 hours. You need to let your emotions (at least somewhat) settle before attempting to analyze what happened.

Step 2: Separate Execution from Design. Ask yourself whether the plan failed because it was poorly designed, or because you didn't execute it consistently. The usual move is abandoning a solid plan over poor follow-through, then designing a worse one because you took the wrong lesson from the experience.

Step 3: Find the Smallest Viable Adjustment. Don't overhaul everything. What's the smallest change you could make that potentially addresses what you learned? If your morning routine fell apart because you tried to wake up 90 minutes earlier, maybe start with 15.

Step 4: Test the Adjustment. Run the modified version for at least two weeks. Give it enough time to reveal its true weak points. One week doesn't usually offer enough data, and one month is too long if something is fundamentally broken.

Step 5: Build Your Failure Resume. Keep a record of what you've tried and what you've learned. The same failures keep repeating when you never collect the data necessary to identify patterns that transfer across every area of their life. **Your failure resume becomes your competitive advantage.**

Progressive Failure doesn't sell well in the Self-Help Industrial Complex because it doesn't promise shortcuts or good feelings. Instead, it demands action. It doesn't offer prescriptive answers, but it'll sure as hell help you find all the ones you're looking for.

It's Going to Feel Like Hell

Let's talk about what Progressive Failure feels like, because this is where many tap out and retreat back to old patterns and identity.

It feels way more like shame than it does "personal development." Like you're going backward, sometimes like you were deluding yourself about who you could become. There's a moment, usually around week three of any serious change effort, where your old self and your new self are wrestling for control. The new behaviors don't feel natural yet, but the old behaviors have begun to feel pathetic. You're caught between two identities, and neither one feels true.

That's the messy middle. That's the Desert from Chapter 5. It's where your commitment gets tested.

That discomfort reads like evidence you're doing something wrong. *After all, our society has been designed to protect you from the very feelings of discomfort you should be using for data points in this journey*. You think feeling bad means you're failing, so you quit. You then retreat to what feels familiar, even when familiar isn't working. You're pressing against the outer walls of your current identity, and your old self is fighting back because change, even good change, feels like a threat to its survival. But that tension isn't failure. That's progress in its truest form, with its sandpaper surface and jagged edges. No shine here.

That shame you're feeling? That's your old identity realizing it's about to be replaced. That frustration? That's the gap between where you are and where you're going, and it's exactly the fuel you need to keep building.

Stay in the discomfort. Don't retreat from it.

The Desert (that messy middle ground where you're no longer who you were but not yet who you're becoming) is where your new identity gets forged.

And at some point, you have to commit with every ounce of your being to who you're going to be in this process.

Are you the archaeologist... Digging through your past, hoping to find something that could explain the "real you" and why change feels so hard? Hoping for a discovery that will finally make everything click? There's nothing "bad" about this work, and every self-development journey possesses archaeology arcs.

Or are you the architect? Because at some point you have to commit to a new story arc of design and action. Of building and refining until you've constructed an identity that can carry the weight of your dreams. The archaeology gave you the ground you're standing on. It did its job, and it did it well. But you can't dig and build at the same time, and this stretch of your life is asking you to build. So which job is this moment asking you to take?

Your Identity Is Under Construction

Every time something breaks, ask yourself what it taught you about what needs to be stronger. Every time you feel like quitting, ask what the next iteration of this looks like. You're not behind, and your failures aren't proof that change is impossible.

What you're constructing in this exact stretch, brick by brick, isn't a feeling. It's a record. The self-reputation ledger from Chapter 3, the one that bottomed out from years of broken promises. The Desert is where it gets rebuilt, because this is the only place the deposits really count. A kept promise on an easy day barely registers because your subconscious expected that one. But a promise you keep when quitting feels completely reasonable, when there's no applause, no visible progress, and every part of you is negotiating for an exit... That's the deposit a bankrupt account can't argue with. That's the construction method. The unglamorous rep you logged in the Desert, on the day nobody, including you, would have blamed you for skipping it.

The loop has a delay built into it. Behavior produces evidence the same day.

Evidence rewrites belief on its own schedule, and that schedule is slower than you want. The Desert is that gap... The stretch where you've already changed what you do, but your identity hasn't caught up to the proof yet. It feels like nothing's working because the part you can feel (the belief, the confidence) is the part that moves last. Keep depositing. The belief is downstream of the evidence, and the evidence is already piling up whether you feel it or not. And on the mornings when everything in you is lobbying to quit the whole project, make the deposit impossible to miss. Feet on the floor. Bed made. The count survives another day.

You're the architect of your own identity. Pick up the pencil. Revise the blueprint. And get back to building.

Because what you're building is bigger than what broke you.

Chapter 13

Borrowed Identity Always Breaks.

WHAT YOU'RE BUILDING: Something that's yours. Copying the people ahead of you got you started, and there's no shame in scaffolding. But scaffolding was never the building. This chapter is where you find out what you've earned versus what you've been renting. Because the rented identity has an expiration date, and life already knows it.

When I first began my coaching practice, I was deeply struggling with imposter syndrome. I'd already been doing the work for years. But now it mattered in a way it never had before. My family's ability to have a roof over their heads depended on my being a great coach that people wanted to work with. So I did what so many others do in this situation. I found some examples of those considered great coaches and I copied the hell out of them.

And it worked for a while. I mastered their most common frameworks and could recite a litany of catchphrases, usually delivered into the silence I'd craft with a perfectly timed (but philosophically deep) question. It didn't matter that these early coaching sessions never really felt like we dug into meaningful territory, because I sure sounded great executing them.

But then a client brought a true crisis to me. Minutes before our session was set to begin, his boss called to let him know their entire department could be axed in an upcoming merger. It wasn't for sure, but serious enough it warranted a heads-up.

He needed me, and in turn I slipped right into the identity of Persona C, "celebrated performance coach to A-listers and Olympic athletes." And within 15 minutes he rightfully called my ass to the carpet. "I need you to drop the shit and be here and be real with me. My world is falling apart." And he was 100% right.

I guess I wasn't nearly as impressive to the world as I sounded in my head (and insecurities).

So I set the clock aside, and I put Persona C back into my closet of borrowed identities. And I then focused on nothing more than serving him and his needs. I stumbled through questions and fumbled my words at times. But what unfolded was the first Lester-led coaching session I ever had in my practice. And copying those coaches? That wasn't the mistake. It's how everyone starts. They were scaffolding, something to climb while I learned to do the real thing. My mistake was staying up on that scaffolding so long I forgot to build anything underneath it.

In the last chapter, we talked about how identity is built through Progressive Failure, through a cycle of testing what works under real conditions. That was about how you build. This chapter is about whose blueprint you're building from. Because most people skip the testing entirely, just like I did. They see someone who's already done the work and built the needed confidence, so they just copy the (visible) outputs. **They replicate the look without building the foundation underneath it.**

And that's the trap.

Belief without evidence is just performance. And performance (no matter how convincing) always has an expiration date. The only question is whether you'll be the one who discovers that, or whether life will handle the reveal for you.

The Leadership Impersonator

I watch this happen constantly in corporate environments, and it follows the same script every time.

Someone identifies an executive they admire. Studies them. How they speak in meetings, the confident pause before answering a difficult question, the language they use when framing a decision. So they start copying it. The buzzwords and the posture, the whole package.

And it works... At least for a bit of time. They get the invitation to the bigger meeting where people smile and nod along when they get the opportunity to speak. So they begin to believe they've cracked something.

Then the first real crisis hits, just like it did with me.

I worked with a guy named Keith. He was a talented manager, even recently promoted to a senior role in his company. And, unfortunately, he was convinced he'd figured out the "leadership thing" by studying the VP above him. He'd collected this man's phrases, fully believed he'd reverse-engineered his decision-making style, and he even practiced the same confident pauses in the mirror. (He told me this later. I kept a straight face. Barely, because I'd worn my own personas years earlier.)

For a few months, it looked like genius. People started calling him "executive material," and he was all too happy to flow along with the (fabricated) momentum.

Then the market shifted within his industry, and the budget cuts came down hard. His team needed to be restructured. He now found himself sitting across from people who trusted him, and he had to deliver news that would change their lives. And instead of finding his own voice for those critical moments, he kept reaching for the VP's.

The result? Corporate-speak when people needed to feel something real. Scripted answers when his team needed someone present in the room. He had learned how to sound like a leader, but he hadn't learned how to be one. Just like me and my early efforts at coaching. Because real leadership isn't about executive presence. It's about making hard decisions with incomplete information. Taking responsibility when things go wrong, and building trust through consistency over time.

You can't borrow those elements of leadership. You earn them, one dilemma and one difficult conversation at a time.

The Identity Shopping Epidemic

We're living through a collective identity crisis disguised as self-improvement.

Social media has turned everyone into identity tourists. You follow the right accounts and find all the right habits to copy. Adopt the right language. And somewhere in that process, you begin to mistake the collection of observations for real personal transformation.

The productivity guru's morning routine. The entrepreneur's mantras about mindset and grind. **We've built an entire economy around selling people someone else's identity, aesthetically packaged as "becoming your best self."**

But identity isn't something you can download. And the most dangerous part is that the borrowed self doesn't feel fake at all. It feels very, very real. At least for a while.

You wake up at 5AM like your productivity hero, and you do feel like you got a ton of stuff done. Then you post insights like your favorite thought leader, and you do feel wise. At least, right up until the moment life asks you for something the scripted performance can't provide.

And there's nothing wrong with learning from the people ahead of you. We all do it, and you should do it too. Imitation is how every skill on earth gets started. The apprentice copies the master. The kid copies the musician she idolizes. Borrowing is the on-ramp. The crime is never getting off it. When you borrow someone else's identity, you're learning the surface behaviors without building the internal infrastructure that makes them sustainable. You're getting the output without doing the work that creates it. You can also think of it like memorizing the answers to a test without understanding the subject. You pass, at least until someone asks you a question that isn't on the cheat sheet.

That infrastructure is the part nobody talks about, because it isn't photogenic. It's the thousand repetitions that nobody watches. The decisions you made correctly when there were real, painful costs involved. The times you held a standard when it would have been easier and more comfortable to let it slide. The failures you didn't explain away, but truly sat with long enough to learn from. That's what creates the internal wiring that makes a behavior stick, or that builds the standards necessary to navigate the difficult patches of life. Not the surface-level action itself, but the experience underneath it that makes you capable of executing it when things get hard.

When you borrow someone else's approach, you skip all of that. And when pressure gets applied, when the situation demands the real thing instead of the imitation, there's no framework underneath capable of weathering the storm.

Why Borrowed Identity Feels So Good (Until It Doesn't)

The borrowed identity trap works because it hijacks your brain's reward system in a way that feels indistinguishable from real progress.

When you copy someone successful, you get an immediate hit of possibility. You feel like you've unlocked something. You might even get external validation, such as people commenting, nodding, responding to the borrowed identity you've artificially constructed. Your brain interprets all of that as progress. But what you're experiencing is the illusion of borrowed progress. A temporary state that depends entirely on maintaining the performance.

And this feels significantly safer than building your own. When you copy someone else's approach and it fails, you can blame the method used in copying the persona. Or you can explain it all away based on circumstance, since the person you copied would surely have figured out a way to pull it off. But you? No need to sit with the possibility that your decision to copy could be to blame.

When you build your own approach and it fails, there's nowhere to hide. That failure reflects on you. Your ideas and instincts. Your very understanding of what works. The emotional stakes feel higher because the responsibility is entirely yours now. So borrowed identity becomes a form of emotional insurance. Psychologists have a name for this, self-handicapping. We arrange a built-in excuse so that if we fail, it never has to mean we weren't good enough. You get to feel like you're growing without assuming the full risks that come with identity development. You get to play at transformation while keeping one foot in the safety of "This isn't really me, I'm just trying their method."

But every insurance policy has a premium. The cost of that emotional safety is that you never build the confidence that comes from succeeding with your own ideas, failing with your own experiments, and learning to trust your own judgment. You're perpetually in someone else's Airbnb, so you never own a property that you get to architect and build.

You can rent confidence, but you cannot fake competence.

Sure, borrowed leadership can look impressive in calm waters. But earned leadership is what keeps you (and the people around you) from drowning when things get chaotic. Borrowed discipline works hard when you're motivated. But earned discipline? It works hardest when you have 186 things you'd rather be doing and none of them are this.

What Earning Looks Like

Earning identity isn't a single event that you either win or lose. It's a process, and you already know its shape. Chapter 5 gave you the Identity Engine (Enthusiasm, Desert, Momentum). Shedding a borrowed identity runs that same engine, just in the hardest conditions. Because before you can build something real, the fake thing has to come down first. That's the only part the Engine didn't prepare you for earlier in the book. The rest, you've already met.

Phase 1 is the Breakdown. The borrowed identity stops working. You find yourself in some incredibly uncomfortable moment, and you realize (or accept) that you've been performing someone else's life, that you've been standing on scaffolding the whole time with nothing built to replace it. This feels like failure, but it's really the possibility of something authentic finally taking root. Unfortunately, most people don't read it that way. They panic, find a new model to copy, and restart the cycle. Different guru, still a borrowed identity.

Phase 2 is the Rebuild. It's the Desert, and this is the ugly part. You're starting from scratch. You feel like a beginner in areas where you used to look competent. It was through imitation, but it still "felt" better than this. Your progress is invisible. The people around you seem to have it figured out (they don't, they're likely performing and your insecurities are convincing you otherwise). And this is exactly where the rebuild usually dies, when your insecurities win. People quit and go back to copying.

What makes the Rebuild phase brutal isn't the work, it's the temptation. The borrowed identity is right there, available to grab. It'd be so easy to snag a quick one-way ticket out of the Desert. You're in a job interview and the old confident script would help you sound impressive. You're at a networking event and the borrowed personality would make you seem more interesting. **Every time you rent instead of build, though, you reinforce the belief that your authentic self isn't enough.** Every performance-instead-of-a-real-attempt delays the moment when your actual capabilities become strong enough to handle what life throws at you.

And the way through the Rebuild phase isn't (more) inspiration. It's evidence. The Identity Engine running on proof instead of inspiration. One small decision made from your actual values instead of someone else's script. One conversation where you showed up as yourself instead of a carefully curated "you." One moment where you failed and didn't immediately reach for someone else's framework to make sense of it all. Instead, you stayed in it and processed the mess. You learned something that's now yours and only yours, because you earned it the hard way.

That evidence accumulates slower than you want it to. But it compounds in a way that borrowed confidence never can, because it's yours. It's something real you can put your hands on. So when the next hard moment comes (and it will), you don't have to reach for a script. You reach back into your own history and find proof that you can handle it. That's the difference. Not fragile motivation. But proof.

Phase 3 is Integration. This is Momentum, the far side of the Desert. And this is the phase most people either don't believe exists or don't recognize when they arrive in it, because it doesn't feel like anything they expected. The expectation is that earning your identity will feel like a destination. Like they'll cross some line and suddenly feel done with the experience and all grown up. But that's not what happens. Not even close.

Integration doesn't announce itself. It shows up quietly, in a moment where you're under real pressure and you notice, almost as an afterthought, that you aren't reaching for anyone else's playbook. You're just responding and figuring it out as you go. And it's working, because you've been building the right infrastructure for long enough that it can now carry the load of crucial moments in your life.

I've watched this happen with clients and it's one of the most striking things to witness from the outside, because the person usually doesn't fully see it themselves at first. Keith (yes, the same Keith who was practicing pauses in the mirror) came back to me about eighteen months after we'd done the hard work of stripping away the borrowed performance. He'd just navigated a brutal restructuring at a new company, and had lost three of his key people in one quarter. Because of this, he found himself rebuilding team trust from near-zero. And when I asked him how he handled it, he paused (a real one) for a bit and said, "I just told them the truth. About what I knew, what I didn't, and what we were going to figure out together." There was no borrowed framework. No mimicked executive presence. Just a man who had spent a year and a half building something real, finally trusting it enough to use it when it mattered most.

That's Integration. You stop comparing yourself to the people you used to copy. You haven't beaten them. That doesn't even matter, as the comparison stopped feeling relevant. You're operating from a different set of coordinates now... Your own. And the strange, quiet confidence that comes from that doesn't need to be performed or announced or posted about. It's just there, underneath everything, holding the structure together.

The identity that emerges from this process is more specific than the borrowed one ever was. More particular. More yours. Less universally impressive on paper, maybe, but unshakeable when tested. Because it was built by you, for you, through real experience that nobody can ever take away.

The Cost of Borrowing

People severely underestimate the true cost of maintaining a borrowed identity.

When you're borrowing, you're always acting for an audience. You have to remember the lines and constantly remain in character. And you better not screw up and forget what borrowed identity you're using as your reference point. You can't have an off day because that might break the act. You also can't ever admit confusion because that breaks character, which means asking for help is off the table. Evolution is impossible since your coordinates are always based upon someone else's idea of success, and they come baked into the borrowed identity.

It's exhausting in a way you can't quite name, because you've confused that exhaustion with the difficulty of personal growth. But it's not growth. It's the cost of maintaining the borrowed identity, and nothing more.

When you earn identity, you're building for yourself. Your confidence doesn't require external validation, since it comes from a track record that you fully own. You engaged the hard things with your full being and you came away a stronger, authentic sense of self. You can have off days because your foundation doesn't depend on how you seem externally. And you can admit what you don't know because your credibility is built on what you do know and what you've done.

Those who have attained real fulfillment aren't the ones who found the right person to copy. They're the ones who stop copying altogether and start the slow, unglamorous work of building from the ground up.

So keep learning from the people ahead of you. But stop trying to live as them. Start asking yourself the question of what works based on your own experiences. What have you learned about yourself through trying and failing. What are your actual strengths, not the ones you think you should have based on who you've been studying.

What kind of person do you become when you stop trying to be someone else?

There's no easy answer to that question. It requires experimentation, and accepting that the picture of yourself you've been working with might be someone else's sketch of who they think you should be.

You owe it to yourself to figure out the answer to that question. Besides, the world doesn't need another false, fragile "success" story. Anyone can toss a rock across Instagram and hit a dozen of them. It needs you to become who you actually are, at your most tested and unshakeable.

That person is built through intention. One hard rep at a time. One honest experiment at a time. Until what you've earned is stronger than anything you could borrow. The scaffolding was always meant to come down.

Because borrowed identity always breaks.

Always.

Chapter 14

Beliefs Are the Blueprint.

WHAT YOU'RE BUILDING: The blueprint underneath everything else. Most of your beliefs were installed before you could question them, by people running on their own fears. You've been building to their specifications ever since. This chapter is where you finally read the plans you've been living from your whole life. And where you earn the right to redraw them.

You're out to dinner, menu open, and you're reading it right to left. Prices first, food second. The server asks about starters and something in you answers before you do. "No, we're good, thanks." You really freaking wanted the calamari. You can afford the calamari. You haven't stressed about money in over a decade. But the menu scan and the "we're good"... None of that consulted you.

Maybe your calamari moment shows up at the grocery store instead, where your hand grabs the store brand on autopilot. Or at the thermostat, where you knock it down two degrees and put on a sweater in your own house, hearing a line about money not growing on trees in a voice that isn't yours.

You didn't make those choices. An underlying belief made them, and it's not one you ever chose to hold. It was handed to you at a kitchen table thirty years ago by someone running on their own fears, and it's been operating like rogue computer code in your head ever since.

Chapter 13 showed you what happens when you build on someone else's designs. This chapter is about the blueprint you've been building on without knowing it... The one that got drawn before you could hold a pencil. You're trying to build the house of your dreams with decades-old architecture plans. Plans you never chose, never questioned, and probably don't even realize you're carrying around.

Your beliefs are the invisible architecture of your entire life. They determine what feels possible, what feels safe, and what feels like "too much" for someone like you. If your current reality feels smaller than your dreams, it's because somewhere along the way you inherited a blueprint that was never designed to build your future.

Think about the standards you've been operating from your whole life (standards being the rules that govern your behaviors). Some you chose deliberately, but most you didn't. And if you've spent any time in the earlier chapters of this book examining the gap between who you say you are and how you actually live, you've probably already noticed the distance between the standards you falsely claim and the ones you actually enforce. It's tough to look at, I get it. You likely have an area of your life with high standards that you're damn proud of. And you should be. But its next-door neighbors haven't cut their yards in months and garbage is spilling from their front porches.

Most people inherit their standards the same way they inherit a religion or a political affiliation... Without consent, little to no examination, and never realizing other options existed. They tolerate it because deep in the foundation, a core belief is quietly running the show. A belief that says *this is what someone like me deserves. This is the ceiling, and there's nothing I can do about it.*

That belief doesn't walk in the front door and announce itself to everyone. Instead, it sits in the corner, unnoticed, and silently determines what feels possible and then quietly rules out everything else.

Your standards are the construction. Your beliefs are the blueprint.

The Blueprint You Never Drew

We're all born into belief systems we never consented to.

Your parents handed you their relationship with money, whether that was scarcity or abundance, fear or entitlement. Across your school years, teachers defined what success looked like and who was allowed to achieve it. Meanwhile, your culture whispered rules about your place in the world before you were old enough to question whether those rules were even true. Many of these beliefs felt like a form of protection at the time. "Don't get your hopes up." "Stay humble." "People like us don't do things like that." Others felt like survival. "Work twice as hard to get half as much." "Don't trust anyone but family." "Keep your head down and don't make waves." And for a while, these beliefs served you. They kept you safe. They helped you navigate a world that felt unpredictable and sometimes even hostile.

The problem is that belief systems don't expire on their own. The one that protected you in one season will quietly suffocate you in later ones. The beliefs that helped a ten-year-old navigating school might be exactly what's handicapping the adult you're trying to become.

This pattern shows up across every background and every culture. It doesn't care about socioeconomic levels. The working-class kid who was told not to get above his raising. The immigrant family's child who learned to blend in and never stand out. The high-achiever from a privileged home who internalized that failure wasn't an option, and then spent thirty years too terrified to try anything with a real chance of going wrong. None of these belief systems were installed by evil people. Most of them were installed by people who loved you, trying to prepare you for a world as they understood it. But they can become prisons the moment you stop examining whether they still apply.

I worked with a talented woman who couldn't understand why she kept sabotaging herself every time she got close to a promotion. She'd work harder than anyone else and deliver exceptional results, then somehow find a way to disqualify herself right before the opportunity became real. After weeks of digging, we uncovered the responsible belief. Her father had been a brilliant, but exhausted man who'd been passed over for promotions his entire career. And he had told her one evening, "In our family, we work hard and get overlooked. That's just how it is for us." She could only remember him ever saying it once, but she had carried it like a familial yoke for over twenty years.

That one sentence became a belief. That belief became a standard she enforced (unconsciously, automatically) every single time success came within reach. She was self-disqualifying because she was honoring a blueprint someone else drew for her.

And I didn't figure this concept out from the outside looking in. I lived it.

I grew up in a house where money was stress. Not a lesson, not a value. Stress. The kind that shows up in loud arguments, guilt trips and a very clear, unspoken message that accumulating it was either impossible or suspect. Actually, both. So when I was in my twenties and making serious money playing poker, I spent it. Immediately. And not even on anything in particular. I tracked my poker sessions meticulously, kept detailed books, understood the math of optimization cold. But the moment real money started sitting in my checking account, something in me got uncomfortable. Like having it there was the problem and the right move was to get rid of it before something bad happened.

I didn't connect these dots for years.

Then I became head of school at a private institution with a tuition structure that exceeded what most colleges cost. We drew savvy families who'd done the research, toured the campus, and were convinced this was the right place for their kid. And I would sit across from them and start apologizing for the price. Talking in circles around it. Hell, most times I was flat-out trying to talk them out of signing. But the school was worth every penny of that bill, and I believed in the mission and what my staff was accomplishing with the kids.

It took a mentor pulling me aside and asking me, "Do you realize you're trying to save these families from a decision they've already made?" I didn't have an answer, as I was clueless that my relationship with money was so toxic I was projecting scarcity onto people who weren't living it. I was trying to rescue them from a belief that was mine and mine alone. But one I'd never chosen. Never questioned. Just... Carried.

So, whose voice is in your blueprint? More accurately, *voices*? Not the polished, conscious version you'd say out loud, but the ones underneath it. There's that one voice that speaks up when an opportunity feels too big or a goal feels too ambitious, when the identity you believe you need feels just slightly out of reach. That voice belongs to someone. It was taught to you at a specific moment in your life, by a specific person operating from their own set of fears and limitations. But it was never meant to be part of your permanent operating system. It was meant to get you through a season of life, almost always an early one. Not define your entire future.

The Inversion Nobody Talks About

There's a pattern I've watched play out hundreds of times across my coaching practice, and it's worth naming directly. This is when someone holds the people around them to higher standards than they hold themselves. They'll fire an employee for consistent tardiness while chronically running late to their own commitments. Sometimes, even with a fresh Starbucks in their hand (seriously). They'll demand excellence from a direct report while accepting half-effort from themselves in areas where they believe no one is watching. They'll push back hard on excuses from others and then extend themselves unlimited grace the moment their own comfort is at stake.

This sounds like simple hypocrisy, but it actually runs much deeper and offers something much more revealing. **Namely, what you're willing to tolerate from yourself is a direct reflection of what you believe you're worth.** When your internal standards are lower than your external ones, it means there's a belief somewhere in your foundational identity that says other people deserve better, from you and from themselves. And you only deserve whatever's left.

That belief won't show up on a performance review. Instead, it shows up in the promises you break to yourself in private. In the morning routine you abandon after three days, or in the opportunity you talked yourself out of before you even put yourself in the running to win it. If you want to find your most honest beliefs about yourself, don't look at what you say. Look at what you accept. Look at the situations you tolerate without complaint. Most of all, look at the standards you hold yourself to at a non-negotiable level. It doesn't matter if other people are around or not. Do you complete that two-hour work block you scheduled for yourself, or quit after the first distraction? Do you eat the healthy meal you packed for lunch today, or ask a coworker to bring a fast food combo back for you? That gap, between what you demand of others and what you actually require of yourself, is the clearest picture of your belief system you're ever going to get.

The standards you enforce in private are the most honest thing about you. And they're being run by beliefs you've probably never examined.

How to Recognize Your Operating System

Self-limiting beliefs don't feel like beliefs at all. They feel like facts.

"I'm just not a morning person." "I've never been good with money." "I'm not the kind of person who speaks up in rooms like that." "Relationships are hard for me." These don't feel like something someone told you. They feel like something you discovered, or like a personality trait. You hold onto them like they're some form of fixed reality. But they're not. They're conclusions you drew from limited evidence, at a time when you had limited options, and then mistook for permanent truth.

The way to start identifying them is to pay attention to your resistance. Not the operational friction of hard things. Hard things are supposed to be hard. The specific flavor of resistance I'm talking about is the kind that shows up when something feels exciting and terrifying at the same time. That collision (*I want this AND something in me is pulling away*) is almost always a belief doing its job. It's the operating system protecting the life it was installed to run. It shows up in the money belief that creates self-sabotage right when income starts to grow. Worse, you were excited when you saw your bank balance growing. At least, until that voice showed up again. It shows up in the leadership belief that keeps you avoiding visibility even when you have valuable ideas. Or in the success belief that forces false either/or choices between achievement and your relationships. In the worth belief that drives the burnout cycles you can't seem to escape, no matter how many times you promise yourself things will be different.

Your current life is a perfect printout of your belief systems. Your conscious intentions get a say in it, but they lose most of the arguments. More of what you do than you'd ever care to admit runs on programming you absorbed long before you could question it. The habits you can't sustain, the patterns you keep repeating and the ceiling you keep bumping up against. These are your default blueprint being enforced. Sadly, you can have exceptional character and still live an artificially-limited life.

So start listening differently. When that internal resistance hits, when you feel pulled to act and immediately notice yourself shrinking (AKA your calamari moment), ask yourself three things: When did I first accept this as true? Who taught me this? And what were they protecting me from that I don't need protection from anymore? The second you recognize someone else's voice in that resistance, you take back the power to choose your own way forward.

Because those aren't your beliefs. They're someone else's fears that you've been carrying so long they started to feel like yours.

Build on Choice

Changing your beliefs is evidence work, and the sequence matters. You can't think your way into a new belief. You act your way there. You replace old beliefs with new ones by building proof. Slowly, deliberately, and through consistent behavior that contradicts the old story. If you've always believed you're bad with money, you start managing it like someone who's good with it, even when it feels awkward and before the results show up. Always believed your dreams are too big for someone like you? Then you take the kind of action that someone with those dreams would take, and you place the first small bet on yourself.

The new belief doesn't come first. The new behavior comes first. And eventually, your identity catches up.

You don't believe you're a writer and then write. You write until you become someone who believes that they're a writer. Writers are formed through shitty first drafts and brutal feedback. You can't believe your way into a manuscript. If you want to be a disciplined person, you don't wait to feel like it. You just get the fuck up before you're ready. You do it tired, until you can feel the discipline growing within. And then the belief you're disciplined follows the action. The research here is early, but it backs this up in a literal way. There's a region of your brain, the anterior midcingulate cortex, that appears to physically grow as you do things you don't want to do. Each hard thing you push through builds your capacity for the next one. Your willpower and innate discipline aren't fixed. You're constructing them, rep by rep.

Your beliefs follow your behavior. Not the other way around.

And that's not new thinking. This was settled long before anyone was scanning brains. Psychologists worked it out decades ago, while trying to explain something strange in their data... People's beliefs about themselves kept shifting to match whatever they had just done. The answer they kept coming back to is almost embarrassingly simple (after the fact). You figure out who you are the same way a stranger would, by watching what you do. There's no inner oracle that prophesied who you have become, or who you'll grow into. There's an observer, always around and always reviewing the footage. You can't dictate to this observer, only show it things. And the less certain you are about who you are, the harder that observer leans on the footage. Which means the wobbliest stretch of an identity rebuild is also <u>its most persuadable moment</u>. This is why witnessing beats believing, all the way back to Chapter 3. The observer is who your behavior loop has been feeding evidence to all along.

But nobody warns you how disorienting this process feels in execution. When you start behaving in ways that contradict your old beliefs, it doesn't feel like growth. It feels like lying. It feels like you're performing an identity that hasn't been earned yet, like you're wearing clothes that don't quite fit. Your self-limiting internal voice, the one built on years of evidence for the old story, will tell you that you're faking it. That you're being inauthentic. That the real you is the one who already knew this wouldn't work.

That voice is not wisdom. You can't obey it. Sure, hear it. Even acknowledge it. But then call it out on its bullshit, and keep moving forward. That's the old blueprint fighting to stay relevant, nothing more.

The discomfort you feel when you act above your old beliefs isn't a sign that something is wrong. It's a sign that your operating system is being rewritten in real time. Most people quit right here, because the internal dissonance feels unbearable. The new behaviors are doable, but people mistake the friction of change for proof that the change isn't real. But the discomfort is the work. Stay in it long enough, keep stacking the evidence, and one day you'll realize the old voice got quieter. It gradually fades away because the new story finally has more proof behind it.

The Blueprint Is Yours to Draw

Yes, you inherited most of your beliefs, but you were never a victim. They were installed before you had a choice. And some of them were born from real pain, real trauma, real systemic challenges that were never your fault. But you're not eight years old anymore. You're not powerless. And you are not required to keep building your life on a foundation that someone else poured. Every belief you're carrying is yours to examine now. Keep what serves you. Demolish what doesn't.

Beliefs are operating systems. Sure, you didn't write your initial code. But you are abso-fucking-lutely responsible for debugging it.

It's okay to outgrow beliefs that kept you safe but now keep you small.

Your beliefs are the blueprint. Everything else (your habits, your relationships, your career, your wealth, your peace) is construction. So, build on truth. Because the person you're capable of becoming has been waiting for you to stop building their prison and start building their life.

Because your future won't be built by the beliefs that got you here. It'll be built by the ones you choose next.

MINI: You're Living in a House You Didn't Build.

You're living in a house you didn't build, decorated with other people's fears, and you've gotten so comfortable in it you've even started telling people it's your aesthetic.

Walk through it and be real with yourself. The belief that wanting more makes you ungrateful... That's been hanging in the hallway so long you stopped seeing it. The voice that says you're too much... That moved in before you were old enough to choose it as a roommate. The one that says people like you don't do things like that... You've repainted around it so many times you've convinced yourself it's purposeful.

But none of it's true. Someone told you it was, and you believed them, and now you're maintaining their anxiety like it's a load-bearing wall.

And not just maintaining it. Defending it. Because at some point, weird as it is, it became "home". You know where everything is. You know which rooms to avoid. You've gotten good at giving tours that make the whole thing come off as quaint and charming. Some of it you've even grown to like, which is exactly what makes it so hard to untangle from YOUR plans for YOUR life.

But comfortable and designed-for-you are not the same thing. And you already know that. You've always known that. The low ceilings aren't new. Eh, you honestly kind of hate them.

And every promise you've broken to yourself is a lien against the property. Every time you talked yourself out of the ask, the application, the leap... Another one. Every Sunday night plan that died by Tuesday morning... Another one. You've been servicing debt on a house that was mortgaged before you ever moved in, making payments on someone else's limitations, wondering why you can never quite get ahead. The bank you owe isn't some external force. It's you. It's the Bank of Self-Reputation from Chapter 3. It's been you the whole time, quietly keeping the running ledger while you rearranged furniture and called it progress.

The people who installed those beliefs aren't coming back to renovate. They built what they built with what they had, and most of them meant well. But none of that changes the fact that you're the one still living in it. Still navigating their floor plan. Still opening doors the wrong way because that's just how the doors open here. Still explaining to guests why the layout is actually fine once you get used to it.

You're not being humble when you listen to those voices. You're not being realistic. You're not honoring your roots or staying grounded or any of the other things we tell ourselves when we choose to rationalize someone else's ceiling over our own potential. You're obeying a recording made by someone who was also too scared to move, who needed the people around them to stay scared too, and who handed you their fear so early you eventually just called it your personality.

That's not your personality. That's their baggage. And you've been unpacking it into every new space you've tried to remodel since.

But you can be the architect now. The whole second half of this book has been about exactly that. Architects don't work from someone else's blueprints. They clear the site. They walk the property with honest eyes and decide what was built for survival versus what should be built for the future. They separate what was designed to contain from what could be designed to expand. And then they ask the question nobody living in an inherited house ever thinks to ask... What would I design if I started from scratch?

Not what would make the neighbors comfortable. Not what would honor the people who lived here before you. What would you actually build, for the life you're actually trying to live, if the lot were empty and the choice was entirely yours?

That question is yours. So is the lot. The only thing left on it that doesn't belong is the structure someone else built before you knew you had a choice.

Tear it down. Build something worth living in.

Chapter 15

Your Real Values Show Up in Hard Choices.

WHAT YOU'RE BUILDING: Your order of operations. Beliefs set what feels possible. Values decide which of two good things wins when you can't have both. Most of yours were inherited the same way your beliefs were, and they're still ranking your choices today. The hard decisions ahead will reveal whose voice is making the call. This chapter makes sure it's yours.

Noel could recite his values with zero hesitation. Personal freedom. Experiences over material things. Our coffee hadn't even made it to the table and he was standing firm that these were the underpinnings for all of his family's decisions.

At the same time, he'd spent the last four months unable to make an offer on a house, because every place he and his wife loved (the smaller ones in neighborhoods that fit the life they were living) kept losing to a voice in his head asking what his parents would think of the square footage. His stated values pulled one way. His decisions, the real ones, the ones that cost something, kept going the other.

That's the gap this chapter is about. Back in Chapter 9, you learned to make hard calls as the person you're becoming instead of the scared one from yesterday. This is where you find out whether you truly know who that person is. Because you can't make decisions as your future self if your values are still on loan from someone else's past. Noel wasn't in the process of choosing a house. He was choosing whose voice got to make the call.

And before you file that dilemma under last chapter's lesson, look closer. Beliefs and values are different layers of the same inheritance. Beliefs are about what's true, and they determine what feels possible for someone like you. Values are about what matters, and they decide which of two good things wins when you can't have both. One sets your ceiling. The other sets your order of operations.

Noel didn't have a belief problem. He knew the numbers on all of the houses worked. Instead, he had an unexamined value, handed across the same kitchen table as his beliefs, still ranking his parents' approval above his own family's desires.

What people say they value and what they actually value are often two completely different things.

I don't say that to be harsh. I say it because I've been coaching long enough to watch highly intelligent, well-intentioned people make choices that completely contradict the values they'd stake their reputation on. And these are never dishonest people. That's what's so difficult about this topic. It happens because they've never gotten into the muck of their life and evaluated the gap between what they say and what they choose. That gap (the space between your stated values and your practiced ones) is where most of your personal frustration, confusion, and quiet self-loathing lives.

Your real values aren't the ones you write on a vision board or list in a journal exercise. They're not the ones you post on LinkedIn or recite in an interview. Your real values are the ones that show up when you're tired, overwhelmed, backed into a corner, and forced to choose between two things that both matter to you.

Because your real values are revealed in conflict, never in comfort.

Your Parents Are Still Making Decisions for You

Back to Noel. He and his wife had seen dozens of places over several months. Every time they found something they liked, they'd agonize over whether to make an offer. Big discussions with trusted friends and family. Late nights running pros/cons scenarios that never quite resolved. The process was exhausting them, and it was starting to put real strain on their marriage, as well.

So I asked Noel to walk me through some of the biggest decisions he and his wife had made over the past few years. Not the house stuff, but all the other stuff. How did they choose where to live when they first got married? How did they decide to have kids? What drove their job changes? How did they pick their vehicles? What did they do with extra money when they had it?

In the beginning, the game feels kind of fun. It's like detective work, tracing the patterns and pulling themes together. But then a blueprint emerges around whose values have been running your life, and whose values have been getting ignored. And it's not so fun anymore. For Noel and his wife, the findings were unmistakable.

Noel's parents had drilled in a core message about home buying. Buy the biggest house you can afford, and don't stress because you're supposed to "grow" into your mortgage as you keep moving forward in life. Real estate is the best investment. His wife's family had their own version of home-buying advice. Location is everything. Best neighborhood, best school system, period. Both families were passing down what they believed to be wisdom. But what they were really passing down were their values. Those shaped by their own experiences and fears, and their own definitions for what success looked like. And before Noel and his wife knew it, they were shopping for a house that would make their parents proud... Not one that would fit who they were and were trying to become.

Good luck baking a cake you'll enjoy eating when there are six chefs in the kitchen, each with their own tastes and methods.

When I mapped out their big decisions over the past few years, there were some other patterns that pointed towards a different story, though. These were clustered around "lower-stakes" decisions, such as what to do on Friday nights or where to invest disposable income. They consistently chose experiences over possessions. They'd rather spend money on travel than on upgrading their apartment. They valued flexibility over security. Adventure and spontaneity over comfort and predictability. Every time they had a real choice and full ownership over the outcome, they chose the same things. Not a few times. Every time.

But in the middle of house shopping, they'd lost the thread. They were getting pulled into square footage and neighborhood prestige. None of which showed up in how they'd been living their lives when they felt a strong sense of agency.

They realized the act of buying a house was never the problem. They'd been deciding with someone else's values.

The most disorienting thing about inherited values is that they don't feel inherited. They feel like yours. They've been with you long enough, repeated often enough, reinforced by enough people you respect, that at some point they became the very water you swim in. You stopped noticing them because you stopped questioning them. And I can't stress this enough, there is nothing inherently wrong with these values. Your parents were trying to protect you from their own wounds. The culture around you was programming you for productivity and conformity long before you could consent. And your community needed you predictable, because tall poppies get trimmed. None of it was cruelty. Just inheritance. Most of it made real sense in the context where it was formed. But when those inherited values are assessed against the architectural plans you have drafted for your future self, they often fail the simple question, "Does this decision-making value serve me anymore?"

Think about what those inherited values really cost in practice.

"Hard work is its own reward" starts as a value about character and discipline. And in a lot of households, it was survival, not philosophy. But when left unchecked that value turned into a workaholic pattern dressed up as virtue. You stay busy to feel worthy and you measure your worth solely by your inputs. And you've been doing it so long that slowing down feels like failure.

"Don't get too big for your britches" starts as a lesson about humility, usually delivered by someone who got knocked down for wanting more and decided the safer message was to want less. But in your life, that same value quietly becomes self-sabotage that looks like modesty, and a ceiling you keep maintaining for yourself without understanding why you even fucking built it.

None of these values started as the problem. The problem is that you never decided whether they were worth keeping for YOUR life. For the story that YOU want to write for YOUR self.

Chosen values look different *because* they're deliberate. "Love is a two-way street" means you expect reciprocity, not just give it. "Effort needs a direction" means you work hard toward outcomes that matter, not just to prove you can grind. "The market decides my worth, not my history" means you price yourself and position yourself based on what you deliver today, not on what someone once attempted to convince you to settle for.

The Values Audit (at the end of the chapter) is about consciously deciding which values you want to carry forward and which ones were never really yours to begin with.

The Gap Between Claiming and Choosing

This is where people get tangled up because they confuse aspirational values with actual ones.

You might say you value individual freedom. But if your last five major decisions were driven by fear, obligation, or what other people expected of you, then freedom is just your personal branding. You like the idea of it, but you haven't truly built your life around it.

You tell your coworkers that family comes first, and you even urge them to take the time needed to take care of sick kids or visit their parents. But your calendar is open for meetings into the late evening hours and you've missed your kid's last four school events. Family isn't a real value for you. It's your personal guilt.

Your real values are found in what you consistently protect when you're under pressure to choose between two "correct" options.

When your stated values and your lived values are misaligned, everything feels harder than it should. You make decisions that look good on paper but feel wrong in your gut. You achieve things that should make you proud but leave you empty. You build a life that impresses others but exhausts you, because you're executing someone else's definition of success without ever realizing that's what you're doing.

I get calls like this all the time. "Should I take this promotion? I'd have to move my family across the country?" "Should I leave this relationship?" These are high-stakes moments. Real life, heavy-ass consequences. And when the client asks me what they should do, my answer is almost always the same question back to them. "What do your real values tell you?"

Most of the time, I get silence. Of course they care about "getting it right." But they've never done the work to figure out what their real values are... So "getting it right" is impossible for them. And in that silence they realize they're throwing darts in a pitch black room. They know what sounds good to everyone around them. But under pressure, when the choice is real and the cost is real, they don't have a framework to stand on.

Once you get clear on your real values... Not the inherited ones, not the aspirational ones, but the really fucking real ones. The actual ones. Then your entire decision-making process changes. The choices don't get simpler. They don't, and they never will. But you now have a framework for evaluating them that truly belongs to you. Yes, life will hand you situation after situation where you're faced with two or more "correct" choices. And making a decision means sacrifice. That process will never be easy. But it can be clear and straightforward. And you don't have to live with crippling guilt, because you know that you made the best decision you could for your future self.

Instead of running endless pros and cons, you should ask one question. Which option aligns better with who I am and what I value? (Exercise at the end of the chapter.) It cuts through the noise. It eliminates the endless cycles of anxiety. It gives you confidence in your choices because you're not making them from emotion or impulse, you're making them from identity. And identity is something you can stand behind.

When Noel and his wife got clear on their real values, the house decision stopped even being a "decision". They went back to looking at smaller places in neighborhoods they loved, kept their housing costs manageable, and used the extra margin to plan a month-long trip to Europe. A year later, Noel told me it was one of the best decisions they'd ever made. Not just because of the trip, but because every major decision since then has been easier because they have a framework. They know what they're living toward. They're connected to their real values.

When someone tried to pressure them into a bigger purchase, they could point to their values and say no with zero apologies. When friends questioned their choices, they didn't need to defend anything. They were living by their own standards, not performing for someone else's expectations.

That's what values clarity buys you. Not an easier life, but a more honest one. And honest decisions, even the hard ones, create far less regret than convenient ones ever will.

CHALLENGE

You've spent this chapter watching what values clarity did for Noel. Now it's your turn, so sit down with a pen and paper and do the work. Now.

List your last five difficult decisions. Not the easy ones. Really drill down to the ones that cost you something. The ones where you had to choose between two things you wanted, or between what you desired and what felt right or obligatory.

For each decision, answer two questions. 1) What did you choose? 2) What did you give up to make that choice?

Then step back and look at the pattern across all five. What did you consistently protect? What were you not willing to compromise on, even when it hurt? What did you consistently sacrifice, even when part of you didn't want to?

That pattern is your real value system. Not what you think you should value. Not what sounds impressive. But what you've been living by.

Now ask yourself the harder question. How many of those values are actually yours, and how many were handed to you by someone who was trying to protect you from their own story?

If your pattern reveals choices driven by fear, obligation, or other people's expectations, know that you haven't failed. If anything, that's just life and part of growing into your own sense of self, and an identity architected by you and no one else. But you did just find exactly where the work is. That's a gift, however painful it might first feel.

Your values run on the same operating system you spent last chapter learning to debug. The only question is whether you keep running someone else's code, or finally rewrite your own.

Chapter 16

You Can't Win the Game If You're Playing the Wrong Role.

WHAT YOU'RE BUILDING: The right you for the moment. Chapter 9 taught you where to spend your energy. This one decides who shows up when you get there. You're carrying more roles than you realize, and the wrong one keeps walking through the wrong door. Your kid doesn't need the executive. The boardroom doesn't need the exhausted dad. The real work lives in the transitions.

You can be elite at everything and still fail if you show up as the wrong person in the moment that matters.

Picture this. A successful father sits at the dinner table with his three young sons. Instead of asking about their day, he's setting "objectives" for their homework completion. Instead of listening to their stories, he's measuring their "performance metrics" from school. Instead of being present with his family, he's running the dinner table like a quarterly business review.

His ten-year-old, though, doesn't need a VP of Sales. He needs a dad.

But this father (a top-performing executive who could close million-dollar deals in his sleep) had brought the wrong identity home. It doesn't matter how successful that identity might be in one area of his life. He was playing the wrong role in the moment that mattered most.

You might read that and think this was a parenting problem. It's heartbreakingly common, but I'll routinely have phenomenal business leaders ask me to help them be better parents. But there's nothing for me to teach them about parenting, per se. They just need to realize they're struggling with a role-selection problem. And the damage it's causing can prove nothing short of catastrophic.

In the last two chapters, we talked about the beliefs running your operating system and the values revealed when things get hard. And this chapter is where those ideas get applied in real time, the moment you walk out of one context and into another. **Because you can have the right beliefs and the right values, but still blow it completely if you show up as the wrong version of yourself.**

That's what role confusion does. It takes everything you've fought to build and then misroutes it.

The Collapse Nobody Saw Coming

That father at the dinner table was one of my coaching clients. He was the kind of person you'd think had it all figured out. Elite sales executive, known throughout the community as a devoted husband and father. He even had basketball skills that would make you swear the guy used to play in the NBA. We had one coaching session on the courts and I said never again. He was the very definition of high-capacity, high-achievement success.

Until everything started unraveling on him.

When he first came to me, he couldn't understand why his performance was slipping across every area of his life. His sales numbers were declining. His wife was frustrated. His kids seemed distant. Despite being more "productive" than ever, his results were collapsing in real time.

"I don't get it," he told me. "I'm doing more than I've ever done. I should be winning everywhere."

But that was exactly the problem.

There was no issue with his capacity, so it was reasonable for him to feel that way. After all, he was more than capable of crushing every one of those areas... In a vacuum. Instead, he was losing because each of those complex areas of his life had created exponentially more role confusion. When I had him map out one typical week, we counted something like 18 distinct roles he was actively trying to inhabit. Sales director, product designer, marketer, coach, mentor, team leader, board member, husband, father, son, brother, athlete... Imagine 18 different people, each with distinct expectations, different energy requirements and widely varied success metrics. And all of them fighting for the steering wheel throughout demanding day after demanding day.

If this is sounding like the balance lie all over again, you're half right. Chapter 9 was about the budget. Where your finite time and energy go, which buckets get filled this season and which get starved on purpose. That problem is real, and he had it. But the budget wasn't what was breaking him. You can allocate every hour perfectly and still fail, because allocation only decides where you show up. It says nothing about who shows up when you get there. Chapter 9 taught you to choose the sacrifice. This chapter is about the person who walks through the door after the choice is made.

No wonder his world was cracking under pressure. He was fundamentally misaligned almost everywhere he was needed.

Role confusion doesn't just hurt performance, either. It erodes identity. **When you try to be all things to all people, you end up being no one to anyone.** Your family gets a distracted form of you because you're still in work mode. Your team gets an overwhelmed shell of you because you're worried about family.

The specific you each of these areas needs, though? He's still lost somewhere out in the parking lot.

The Role Confusion Trap

When people hear the word "role" they think of something actors do. Act out what's needed, then take a bow. But this couldn't be further from the truth. Roles are complete identities you step into, each with its own mindset, energy, and behavioral expectations. Think of them like mini-yous that all combine into the larger whole. Like Voltron. Which is kind of kick ass.

When you're in "Sales Director" mode, you're strategic, results-focused, direct. You think fast and move even faster, always pushing for greater outcomes. You're the red lion of Voltron that makes up the right arm, holding the sword. But when you're in "Dad" mode, you're patient, nurturing, and always present. You know the parent you want to be, you've thought on this for years. You want to listen more than you speak and prioritize connection over efficiency. You're the yellow lion of Voltron, and you're the sensitive backbone of the team.

The challenge everyone finds in detangling themselves from role confusion is that each one demands an entirely different version of you. And you cannot run 18 of them simultaneously without your internal computer crashing. For example, every role has its own emotional operating temperature. Sales Director runs red: competitive, urgent, results-focused. Dad runs yellow: patient, nurturing, protective. Athlete runs blue: disciplined, process-oriented, long-term focused. When you're recklessly attempting to rapidly switch between those temperatures without any transition time, your internal thermostat goes haywire. You end up bringing Sales Director heat to bedtime stories. Dad warmth to quarterly reviews. Health-based discipline to marriage tensions.

At best you just end up facing decision fatigue in areas where you thought you had clarity. And this is bad enough since you'll find yourself paralyzed by choices that should be automatic and exhausted by conversations that used to energize you. That's often the best-case scenario. For most, though, your performance levels begin dropping off in critical areas of your life. Your coworkers are wondering where the action-oriented leader has gone, as your team feels pulled in a million directions by your confused and ever-changing presence. Your teenage kids make it known they hate eating dinner with you since it feels like an interrogation instead of family time. And your workout partner doesn't exactly feel like they have a partner anymore. You show up physically, but they design all the workouts and fight to keep the motivation and pace going.

This is why highly capable people often feel like they're failing everywhere simultaneously. They have a case of identity whiplash, not incompetence.

But once you feel your performance slipping, things only get worse. You take the role you feel best at and begin to brute force it onto everything else in your life. My client was exceptional as a sales director, since he knew how to set targets, create urgency, measure performance, drive results. Those skills had made him who he was in his career, a well-known salesperson and leader. But when the pressure mounted, he brought that same energy home. And to his friendships. And to his parents. Everywhere.

Same hammer. Everything a nail to him. And everything kept breaking.

People don't even realize they're doing it. They just know what works in one context, and they keep reaching for it for all of the others. But your 8-year-old child doesn't need a sales director. He just wants a dad that'll get down on the floor and play Legos with him, even if he's in a suit and tie. Your wife doesn't need a performance coach (yeah, this one hits painfully close to home for me). She needs a husband who will just sit and shut up and let her vent as long as needed about how her boss is a total asshole. She doesn't want to be fixed, she just wants a husband that's empathic and present. And your aging parents sure as hell don't need an entrepreneur pitching them on all the possibilities for their future if they would just consider selling the old family home. They just fucking want a son who shows up with love and attention, and who unconditionally honors their reality. He doesn't have to even agree with it. Just honor it.

Your various roles can inform the others, but they can't replace them. The discipline that has kept you in great shape as you've gotten older, that can help out your approach to parenting. But you need to apply that discipline towards being consistently present and protective, not to turning your kid into a training project. The strategic thinking that makes you a great executive can enhance your marriage, but you use it to prioritize connection, not to optimize your spouse. Same core strengths. Completely different applications, completely different identities.

Glass Roles vs. Rubber Roles

Once we mapped all of his roles, I introduced the concept that became his lifeline. Glass roles versus rubber roles. You've already used this framework (back in "Balance is a Lie") to sort your seasonal priorities. Here, the application shifts from what you're working on to who you're *being*. Glass roles are the ones you cannot afford to drop. If you fumble them, they shatter and the consequences are essentially irreversible. Fractured relationships. Missed milestones. Permanent damage to what matters most to you. Rubber roles can survive the drop. They bounce, so they can be paused or even delegated, all without lasting damage. They may feel important, but they're not essential in this season.

For my client, being a dad was glass. So was being a husband, as his marriage was feeling the strain of months of pressure. His sales performance? Also glass, because it funded everything else in his world. But the three basketball nights a week at the YMCA? Rubber. His board member position at a local non-profit? Rubber. He loved these things, for sure. But through the lens of buckets and roles, he knew he had to get real with himself before the glass in his life shattered.

Your glass and rubber roles can evolve as your life's context changes. When you have young kids, parenting is glass and networking is rubber. When you're building your career, performance is glass and weekend social obligations are rubber. When your parents are aging, family support is glass and side projects are rubber. The key is making a conscious decision about what's glass in this season, not trying to make everything glass simultaneously.

Not all roles deserve the same level of investment from you. Stop trying to bring your A-game to roles that don't even require you to show up.

But knowing which roles are glass is only half of it. **Glass roles don't shatter because you stopped caring about them. They shatter in the handoff, in the moment you're supposed to become the father but you're still being**

the director. So the work isn't just naming your glass roles. It's building the transitions that protect them. You don't get to be present for what matters most by accident. You design it.

The Work Is in the Transition

Nobody falls apart "inside" the role. That's where you feel the greatest amount of stress because you're within the emotional moment. But it's in the transition between roles where it all comes apart. My client loved being a father. He just never stopped being a sales director long enough to become one. He would walk through his front door still mentally filing a debrief on the client call he'd just finished, probably from the driveway. He'd sit at the dinner table with his body at home and his mind still at the office.

I knew that if our sessions were focused on managing his time (where most experts would go), things would only get worse for him. Now we would be creating expectations for results without underlying systems to address the root problem. We needed to manage his identity transitions.

It started simple. A sticky note on his steering wheel that read, "Dad, not Director." A conscious decision, made in the driveway, to leave the professional stress in the car. The stress was real and he needed to honor that, so he would be sure to dump all his thoughts onto a notepad before opening the car door. His brain knew, now, it would be waiting for him there later in the evening. Three breaths before walking through the door. He changed clothes when he got home. Literally took off the executive identity. Put his phone in a drawer during family time. Collectively, these were signals to his brain, to his nervous system, to the people waiting for him inside, that the dad and husband they needed had arrived home to them. Every one of those rituals existed to protect a glass role. The intentionally designed transitions made this possible.

That's the difference between being present and being passive. Passive means you drift from one context to the next and hope your brain catches up. Present means you make a deliberate choice about what role is walking through that door.

Try it out for yourself. Think about all your transition points throughout the day. Before you hit your next one, stop and ask "What role does this next moment need me to fill? Not what role I think or feel would win, but which one is actually needed?" It's the same call you've been making since Chapter 9, just pointed at a doorway instead of a sacrifice. Which version of you does this moment need, the one you're building toward or the one that's easiest to be right now?

Even when you've built strong transitions, life will test them. A work crisis hits during family dinner. A kid calls mid-meeting. You don't always get to transition on your own terms with clean introspection. When these occur, the move isn't to pretend it isn't happening. It's to name it. "I need to shift into work mode for 20 minutes, then I'm fully back." I would even share that script out loud with those impacted, such as your wife and kids at home or your teammates at work. When people first hear this in coaching, they feel like that would mean failing. But that's your own insecurities speaking up. What's happening in the real world? You're honoring both roles instead of half-assing both simultaneously. That's the system working.

And when you catch yourself playing the wrong role (because you will), just reset. "Sorry, I was still in work mode. Let me try that again as your husband." People appreciate honesty far more than they appreciate a perfect performance. You would be stunned at how this admission can defuse the situation. And in turn you give those around you permission to reassess their own role of choice and to reanchor their presence as well.

My client stayed the same high-capacity guy with the same ambitions. He just stopped letting his roles run into each other. And in turn, his wife got her husband back and his kids had their dad. All of him. His sales recovered, because he could finally be all-in on his professional roles when required. And the community visibility he'd been clinging to so pridefully? It leveled out, and for the first time that didn't feel like losing. He'd decided it was rubber this season, and he meant it.

CHALLENGE

This is your framework for this season.

Start by listing every role you've inhabited in the past seven days. Be honest about how much energy, attention, and identity each one demanded. No hiding behind "just 15 minutes".

Then classify them. Glass roles shatter when dropped. Rubber roles bounce when you're ready to pick them up again. Be ruthless about which is which right now, in this season, not based on how you wish things were.

Next, run an energy assessment. For each role, ask yourself whether you're bringing the right energy to that identity, or whether you're brute-forcing your strongest role onto contexts where it doesn't belong.

Then design one transition. Just one. One intentional cue that helps you step into your most important role with clarity and presence. A song. A ritual. A question you ask yourself in the car before walking inside. Start there.

Finally, give yourself permission to be imperfect in the rubber roles while you master the glass ones. You're not a failure for letting rubber roles bounce. But you’re an absolute fool if you drop the glass ones while performing for an audience in the rubber ones.

Chapter 17

The Last Lie.

WHAT YOU'RE BUILDING: Nothing. For once, the construction is done. This chapter is about moving in. Living inside the identity you've built instead of maintaining a polished lie for whoever might be watching. You've kept yourself show-ready for an audience that was never going to make an offer. That ends here. And the exhale on the other side is real.

You typed the reply an hour ago. Two honest sentences about why someone's idea won't work. You've rewritten them four times since... Softening the open, adding an exclamation point, trading "I disagree" for "Just playing devil's advocate here!" By the time you hit send, there's nothing left in the message but passivity with a fresh haircut.

Not sure if you've ever sold a house before, but there's a concept in the process called "show-ready." This means your house is ready for a potential buyer to come walk through it. Which also means this term has been responsible for more family arguments than "what to watch tonight" could ever hope to match. There is no shortcut to show-ready. It's not like you can just toss all the loose stuff (the stuff a normal house has laying around) into the closets, because you know in your soul the shoppers are going to open every door and drawer to look through all your crap. However long your home is on the market, you have to keep your house within 15 minutes of a show-ready state. Okay, 30 if you're cool with living dangerously.

Because when you get that text notification that a potential buyer is in the neighborhood and wants to swing by in 45 minutes? Shit just got real.

As someone who's been through the selling process three times, it totally fucking sucks. Beds made like nobody sleeps in them. The shower glass wiped down after every shower. Seriously. When the water turns off and you have to reach for the squeegee AGAIN, another angel loses its wings. No bacon, because buyers don't like the smell of your life. Bacon. AKA the meat of the gods. And then the realtor tells you the last one... Take down the family photos. Buyers need to be able to imagine themselves living here. So you box up your family's faces and put them in the garage, and you pretend like you don't exist for the comfort of others.

It's exhausting in a way that's hard to explain to anyone who hasn't done it. It's technically your home, but you're not really living there. You're just maintaining a property for the approval of strangers who might walk through at any moment.

But at least when you sell a house, there's a closing date.

Now back to that email from a few minutes ago. Take a hard look at your opinions, the ones you swapped out for curtains so neutrally colored that no one would ever notice them. Forget the email, and let's look at your life as a whole. Preferences boxed up and stored away so nobody trips over them. The personality you never cook with, just in case some random stranger might not like the smell. You've been running a permanent open house in your life. And the property is yours. You drew the blueprint. You did the hardass work of building the home. But you still won't take your clothes out of the suitcases and just move in. You won't throw that god forsaken squeegee away and just let a shower be a shower. And you won't cook the fucking bacon. How can you go on another day without bacon?!

Because you're living in perpetual worry that someone will see you for YOU. For the identity that you designed. That you built.

This is not role confusion. It runs even deeper than that, to the core of who you are. A role is a version of you that you choose, deployed because the moment needs it. Staging is an inauthentic self that you maintain, so that anyone who walks through your life feels comfortable. You can set a role down when you leave the room. But the staging we're talking about now follows you everywhere, from the shower to your bed while you're staring at the ceiling at 2AM with a knot in your stomach you can't put words to.

So let me say the thing your nervous system has been waiting sixteen chapters to hear.

You're not broken. You're not lost. You're not having a breakdown. You're exhausted from keeping yourself show-ready for people who were never going to buy into your identity anyways.

The Identity Hijack

Somewhere along the way, you started optimizing for approval instead of authenticity. You learned to perform the identity that got the early promotions. The one that kept the peace at family dinners. The you that didn't rock the boat, ask uncomfortable questions, or want inconvenient things. You became really good at being who everyone else needed you to be.

And it's killing you.

When your behavior consistently contradicts your core identity (when who you are on the outside doesn't match who you hunger to be on the inside) your brain goes to war with itself. It creates psychological tension that shows up as anxiety, burnout, depression, or that soul-crushing feeling that nothing you do actually matters.

You're living someone else's life and calling it your own, and most people don't even realize it's happening. They think this is just what "growing up" looks like. So you compromise a little here, adapt a little there, and eventually you wake up one day wondering who the hell you've become. When every part of your identity has been tweaked for others, you're left with an unrecognizable whole. You look in the mirror and see a stranger wearing your face. You go through the motions of a life that technically belongs to you but feels like it was designed by committee. And those achievements you *feel* like you should be chasing? They don't make you proud. They make you feel ever more empty. That emptiness, though? It isn't weakness. It's your real self banging on the door, screaming to be let out.

And the worst part about identity-pretending is how good society is at reinforcing the behavior. You get rewarded for being agreeable. Promoted (early in your career) for being "low maintenance." Praised for being the one who never complains and never pushes back. So you keep doing it. You keep being the self that other people find convenient. You bury the parts of your personality that might be "too much". Your creativity, your opinions, the very edge that makes you... You. You silence the perspectives that might create conflict around some groups of people, but then never remember to switch them back on later. Healthy conflict, the kind that deepens relationships and builds real trust? Not for you. It's almost impossible to disagree with you, after all.

You shrink your dreams to fit other people's comfort zones. And then you wonder why you feel like you're suffocating.

The identity you've been performing isn't just exhausting, it's fucking expensive.

Every day you spend being someone else is a day you're not investing in who you actually are. Every time you choose what's expected over what's authentic, you're making a withdrawal from your self-reputation. Enough withdrawals, and your voice goes quiet. And eventually, you go bankrupt. Not financially. Spiritually.

You lose touch with what you actually want, what you actually believe, what actually matters. Because you've been so busy being who everyone else wants you to be that you've forgotten who YOU are underneath all the performance.

I Know Because I Did It Too

I want to stop here for a second, because this isn't a chapter I can write from the outside as if I've always maintained a healthy distance from pretending.

In my early 30s, I had constructed a life that looked pretty damn impressive to anyone walking by. I was a respected leader in education. I was working through my doctorate at a prestigious school. I had an amazing and supportive wife, and our family had just grown with a beautiful daughter. I was in great physical shape and took pride in my training. We lived in a sought-after zip code.

Anyone looking in would see a smiling guy waving from the window, just hoping someone would come in to tour our home. Everything was great! My check-ins with my VP were always positive. Everyone on my team could count on me being available 24/7. Calls with friends were full of nothing but laughs. My professors loved my level of engagement and the work I was producing.

But... The math wasn't mathing. I was giving 60 hours a week to my job, and at least 30 to my doctorate program. I'd toss another 10 at workouts. And my wife was struggling through severe post-partum depression, but I couldn't open up about that with anyone. Depression doesn't make for positive house tours. I tried to make it home for lunch every day I could, pick up as much of the cooking and cleaning as possible, change every diaper I could get to.

I was sleeping around 3 hours a night, running on nothing but a cocktail of coffee, 5-Hour Energy, and self-deception.

And I ended up in the hospital for two weeks when my stomach stopped emptying into my intestines. I'll spare you further details, as it's disgusting. But just know I had a vacuum tube inserted through my left nostril and into my stomach for almost a week. I was quite literally on death's door when my wife got me to the hospital, and I eventually left with no diagnosis. Every test imaginable, and my team of doctors could only offer educated guesses. And the one they were most confident about? I had endured a physical breakdown caused by an extreme amount of stress.

Over the next few months, though, something crazy happened. My wife shared her struggles with family and close friends, who dove into supporting us. Just like they always would have if they had just known. My leadership team at work stepped up and rocked leading the school while I took it easy for a while. You know, just like they would have if I had just let them. My doctoral cohort ensured I had reading notes to stay up to date in my classes. I learned they had formed teams to divide and conquer the mountains of reading assignments, and they added me in. Just like they would have from day one, if I had just asked.

It took a hospital bed to take my "show-ready" house off the market. And when the staging came down (because I literally could no longer physically keep it up) nobody ran. The people who mattered walked through the real thing, mess and all... And they moved in with us. That's the part the performance never let me see. Strangers tour staged houses, but YOUR people move into real ones. The support systems we needed were all just one honest sentence away. Our family and friends, my leadership team, my cohort. They were all standing outside a staged house waiting to be let into the real one.

The Performance Tax

I dropped the superman act because my body dropped it for me. You shouldn't have to learn it the way I did. The performance runs a tax, and it compounds quietly until the bill arrives all at once.

Your brain wasn't designed for constant code-switching, especially the kind associated with identity incongruence. Research shows that your brain can't tell the difference between "I'm pretending to be someone else" and "I'm in danger." So it runs the danger program. All day. Cortisol, nervous system activation, the body's full threat machinery. I know, because mine ran that program until it put me in a hospital bed. You're attacking your core identity every day you refuse to be yourself.

Think about what that costs you, all day every day. You're calculating what response will get the best reaction before you speak, and you're perpetually editing your natural instincts to fit what you think other people are expecting. You're always on the lookout for opinions to suppress that might create friction with whoever is in the room with you this moment. You're keeping track of which iteration of "yourself" you showed to which people, always actively managing the gap between your public image and your private reality. Your real personality? You can't remember the last time it was seen in public, since constantly assessing whether it might be "too much" led to you permanently leaving it locked away in the broom closet.

That's systematic self-abandonment, and it cuts soul-deep.

The compound interest of inauthenticity is brutal. Each day you spend managing a false identity, you get further disconnected from knowing what you actually want. You're teaching yourself in real time that who you are isn't really acceptable. And each decision made based on what others expect erodes your ability to trust your own judgment. You're running two operating systems simultaneously, who you are and who you're pretending to be. No wonder you're exhausted. You're living in perpetual split-screen mode.

But before you can stop pretending, you have to see where you're doing it. Because these patterns have been running for so long, most of them feel completely normal and more like personality traits instead of survival strategies. They're not. Just like they weren't for me.

Pay attention to your language. "Whatever you think is best." "I'm fine with either." "You're the expert." "I don't really have a preference." Those aren't collaborative phrases, they're disappearing acts.

Pay attention to your body. Tension in your jaw when you smile and agree with something you don't actually believe. That hollow fatigue after social interactions where you felt "on". The flat feeling after accomplishing something that should have made you proud, and didn't. The sense that you're watching yourself from the outside instead of living from the inside.

Pay attention to your relationships. People who seek you out for advice but seem strangely incurious about your struggles. Friends who love your "positive energy" but have never seen you angry, disappointed, or uncertain. Professional relationships where you're valued for being "easy to work with" but never consulted for your actual perspective.

And the most telling sign of all is that persistent feeling of "nobody really knows me" even when you're surrounded by people who claim to appreciate you. They don't. Not really. Because you've been showing them a character instead of a person.

When You Start Showing Up Real

Once you recognize the performance, you'll face the emotional reality of changing it. And it's messier than most people would even expect.

The first thing you'll feel is guilt. When you stop automatically saying yes to everything and stop performing the identity that keeps others comfortable, people will notice. And most of them will push back. Others will seem confused or disappointed. And you'll feel like you're letting every single one of them down. But you're not. At all. You're letting down their expectations of who you should keep pretending to be. That's a different thing entirely.

Then comes the grief. And I want to sit here for a minute, because this part gets skipped over in most conversations about authenticity. People want to rush to the relief, because that's the happy part of the story. But the grief is real, and it deserves acknowledgment. You'll start doing the math on lost time. The years you spent being someone else. The opportunities you didn't pursue because they didn't fit your performed identity. The elements of yourself you kept locked away because you weren't sure the world could handle them, or even that you deserved to express them. The relationships that now feel fake because they were built on a foundation of your own invisibility, where people loved a form of you that you quietly knew wasn't true.

You may feel anger, too. At the people and environments that rewarded the performance, at the culture that made you believe shrinking was the safe choice, at yourself for going along with it for so long. All of that is fair. Feel it. Name it. Don't skip it in your rush to get to the good part.

Because what follows the discomfort is real. Not the manufactured relief of a self-help "find yourself" weekend seminar, but a genuine soul-deep exhale from finally being able to stop managing your image every waking moment. The energy that comes back when you're not constantly monitoring and editing yourself. The strange lightness of walking into a room and not immediately calculating who to be.

And the relationships... The ones that deepen when people start seeing who you actually are, that alone makes the pain worth it. These relationships become deeper because you've finally become more real to these people, not because you're magically more impressive in their eyes. And some people won't make that transition with you. People that you thought had your back and truly cared for you. But they didn't. They cared for the comfort you brought them at the cost of your own.

Not everyone will love the real you. But the ones who do will love you for the right reasons. And for the first time in a long time, you'll be able to love yourself for the right reasons, too.

The Transformation Myth

At this point, you might be bracing for the renovation... The big transformation that belongs on HGTV. The gut job, the "new" you. I have good news for you, though. There's no construction left to do. You're not becoming someone else. You're becoming someone real, and that person is already standing in the house. You don't need a different career, a different city, or a different set of contacts in your phone. You don't need a different house at all. You need to move into this one. Take the photos out of the garage and put them back on the walls. Say the sentence you actually mean in tomorrow's meeting. And for the love of all things holy, cook the fucking bacon. Let the smell of your life back into the rooms.

The goal isn't to become someone new. It's to stop being someone fake.

Start with one honest question. What parts of me have I buried to keep other people comfortable? Sit with it. Preferably write it down so you can come back to it a few times and add as needed. The answer won't come all at once, and that's fine. Just start being honest about where the performance shows up in your language and your relationships.

Then start impossibly small. Not "quit your job and move to Costa Rica" small. Actually small. One honest opinion in today's meeting instead of the reflexive agreement. One boundary this week that disappoints someone but honors your energy. Nothing dramatic, just a quiet "I can't do that." One conversation where you share what you actually think rather than what lands well. One preference you stop keeping to yourself because you don't want to seem high-maintenance.

You built false identities in an effort to earn love, safety, and status. You paid the cost of performing your own unworthiness. And somewhere along the way, you started believing that life was just... This.

It wasn't. It never was.

You're not broken. You never were. You just forgot who you were underneath all the performance. That's fixable, and it doesn't start with a dramatic reinvention. It starts the next time you tell the truth when a comfortable lie is available.

MINI: Your Past Called. Let It Go to Voicemail.

Your past is a needy ex that won't stop texting.

It shows up at 2AM when you're trying to make a decision, reminding you of all the times you got burned. It whispers sweet nothings about how safe and comfortable things used to be. It guilt-trips you about loyalty and consistency, like changing your mind is some kind of betrayal instead of, you know, growth.

And just like that needy ex, you keep responding. Every time. You read the message, you feel the pull, and before you've even thought about it you're typing back, explaining and justifying, relitigating decisions you already made. All the while, a different conversation sits waiting for you to finally start it.

What you haven't figured out yet (because it's easier not to) is that you're not even protecting your past. You're protecting your story about your past. The narrative you constructed about who you are, what you're capable of, what you deserve. That story worked great when you were 15 and scared of everything. It's working significantly less well now that you're supposed to be, I don't know, a functioning adult with actual options available to you.

But stories are addictive. Especially the ones that make us feel safe and predictable. Especially the ones we've been telling ourselves for so long they stopped feeling like stories and started feeling like facts.

The story about why you can't take risks ("Remember what happened last time?"). The story about why you can't disappoint people ("That's not who I am"). The story about why you can't want more ("I should be grateful for what I have"). You've reread these so many times they stopped sounding like choices you made and started sounding like the truth about you. And the wild part is you'll defend them, hard, like protecting them is protecting yourself. It isn't. It's just answering the same old text one more time.

Meanwhile, your future self has been calling. Not texting, but calling. The kind of call that actually requires something from you. And it keeps ringing and ringing because your hands are already busy typing out replies to a conversation that should have ended years ago.

That version of you, the one who could handle bigger challenges, create real impact, live aligned with your values instead of your fears... It isn't asking for a lot. Just some of the energy you're burning responding to notifications from a chapter that's already closed. Just a fraction of the attention you're pouring into a text thread that should have been retired a long time ago.

The longer you go on ignoring the call the easier it gets to never pick it up. That's how this works. Avoidance compounds. Every day you don't pick up, letting it ring starts to feel like a reasonable choice. Comfortable. Stagnant. Safe.

Growth always feels like betrayal to the parts of you that aren't ready to evolve. Your old identity will throw a tantrum. A convincing one, because it knows every one of your weak spots. It will make wanting more feel ungrateful. It will make changing your mind feel like a character flaw. It will dress your fear up in the language of integrity and call it loyalty.

But it's not loyalty. It's just fear with better PR.

Wanting more doesn't mean you were wrong before. It means you've been paying attention.

Your past had its moment. It got you here. That was always all it was supposed to do. You don't have to delete the thread, either. But you do have to stop writing back.

And when you stop, your past will do what needy exes always do once the texts quit landing. It'll call.

Let it go to voicemail.

And finally pick up the other call.

Chapter 18

The Work Evolves. It Never Ends.

WHAT YOU'RE BUILDING: The YOU that maintains all of it. The frameworks are built. The house is real and you're living in it. What's left is the part nobody puts on a book cover. Every new level of your life will open with its own silence and ask for new proof. You'll never be finished. By the end of this chapter, you'll understand why you wouldn't want it any other way.

You made it here.

You've done both halves of the work by tearing down the lies you were living inside and starting to build something real in their place. You understand that identity isn't something you find at a weekend seminar or in a personality assessment. It's something you design and construct, one unforgiving rep at a time.

You know that confidence comes from evidence, not affirmations. That your perspective shapes your reality more than your circumstances do. You've learned that Promise Debt is real, and the only way out is through. That borrowed identity cracks under pressure, but the identity you earn through honest work gets stronger the more it's tested. You understand the difference between the role life requires of you and the role you keep defaulting to out of habit. And in the last chapter, you gave yourself permission to stop performing an identity that was never yours in the first place.

That's the whole architecture.

I already know what you're thinking. You're somewhere between relief and restlessness, and the question forming in the back of your mind is some variation of "When does it end? When do I get to stop rebuilding and just be the person I've become?"

And, as always, I'm going to shoot you straight.

Never.

Before you close the book, stay with me. Because "never" isn't the punishment it sounds like. It's the thing that makes all of this worth doing.

The Finish Line You've Been Promised Doesn't Exist

We live in a culture that packages "arrival" like it's an actual destination. Like somewhere after hard work and around a metaphorical finish line, there's a moment where you exhale and say "I made it" and everything after that is just coasting on the reward. It's why many of my clients first reach out. The huge two-year run at work ended after they treated it like a finish line, and now they're on the verge of losing the job that past effort built.

You chase the degree as if it's going to objectively announce to the world you're educated, or you fight for the promotion as if it will somehow prove that you've mastered your career and industry. You finally hit the goal you've been grinding toward. The business crosses the threshold. The marriage happens. You expect to feel complete... Transformed... Like you've crossed into a new volume of your life.

Instead, though, you feel restless. Sometimes hollow.

You confused reaching a milestone with becoming someone capable of holding what you'd built. The milestone was real. But the transformation you expected to feel on the other side of it wasn't waiting there for you. It's not a switch that gets flipped once you've hit the achievement. And neither do those achievements automatically extend to the other areas of your life.

The executive who spent a decade building credibility in the boardroom arrives in his own kitchen with none of it. A decade of commanding senior leaders builds zero evidence that he can connect with a teenager who's shutting him out. Different arena, empty account.

And even the same arenas of life can bring new challenges through new contexts. The person who finally mastered their individual finances faces entirely new terrain when building shared financial goals inside a marriage. The discipline that made you an aggressive saver as a single person requires a completely different application when the person across from you has their own history with money, their own fears, their own logic, their own vision of what security looks like.

The athlete who dominated at one level quickly finds out that the work ethic that made them exceptional there is just the entry fee at the next one.

Past evidence can get you to the starting line of something new. It can give you confidence that you've handled hard things before. But it doesn't guarantee you can handle what you haven't faced yet. Every new level demands new proof. Your previous work still counts, of course. But each new challenge tests different capabilities, exposes different weaknesses, and requires a version of you that doesn't exist yet.

And when you convince yourself "you've arrived"? You stop doing the work that got you there. You start coasting on who you were instead of building who you need to become for the next level. You rely on old evidence instead of creating new evidence. That's when things start eroding. The relationship that felt solid begins to crack because you stopped contributing to it. The career that was climbing now plateaus because you stopped developing. The health you built deteriorates because you stopped prioritizing the choices that created it in the first place.

The self-reputation doesn't travel, but the ability to build one does. You show up in the new arena with an empty account and a proven method, because you've filled one before from zero. That's the difference between starting over and starting again.

Growth Doesn't Move in a Straight Line

Most people picture transformation as a straight line moving up and to the right. You start here, you work hard, you make progress, and eventually you reach the top. Clean. Simple. Predictable.

But that's not what actually happens. Not even close.

Real growth moves in a spiral.

It's the same loop from the introduction. Behavior, evidence, belief, repeat. Only now each pass leaves you one level up, where the whole thing begins again on ground you haven't tested.

You build self-trust in one domain. Say your health routine. You prove to yourself that you can keep promises about your body through workouts, sleep, nutrition, recovery. You accumulate evidence. Your confidence grows. The former you who used to negotiate with their alarm clock begins to feel like a stranger.

Then life presents something new. A leadership role. A major relationship transition. And suddenly it feels like you're back at the beginning. But you're not. The self-trust you built around your health routine just doesn't automatically transfer to running a team or navigating a marriage in crisis. You have to build new evidence. Prove yourself in unfamiliar territory and develop capabilities you've never needed before. Yes, when you hit a new level that tests you in ways you haven't been tested, it can feel like you've lost all the progress you made. Like you're back to being the uncertain, unproven self you thought you'd left behind. But it's all an illusion, and you haven't really regressed. You've spiraled upward (think "earned") to a level that requires a new version of you. Because every new level brings it's own Desert for you to navigate. The difference is that this time you know what the silence is... The sound of deposits landing before the belief catches up.

Imagine a spiral staircase. Every time you come back around to a similar-looking challenge (doubt, resistance, that feeling of being in over your head), you're one level higher than you were before. The view looks familiar, but you're operating from a different base. You have evidence from previous cycles that you can handle hard things. You have frameworks you've tested. You have self-reputation you didn't have the last time you felt this way. And the pattern runs the same at every level. A new challenge appears, something you've never faced before, something that exposes a gap in who you currently are. The version of you that handled the last thing isn't equipped for this one. YET.

But you have a blueprint that works and your Identity Engine knows the process forward. You build new evidence. You test approaches. Some of them fail. You learn what doesn't work. You adjust, try again, and slowly, through the kind of Progressive Failure we've talked about across this entire book, you build competence in new territory. You prove to yourself that you can hold this, too.

And then, just when you've gotten comfortable, life presents the next thing. Something bigger. Something that requires more. And the spiral UPWARD begins again.

This is progression, not punishment. Nothing worth holding lives at the bottom of the staircase.

The only alternative would be to remain exactly where you are forever. But stagnation isn't really an option. Even when you try to stay still, the world keeps moving around you. Relationships evolve and demand new things. Industries shift and require new skills. Your body ages and requires different care. The people depending on you grow and need different elements of you.

You're either spiraling upward through new challenges, or spiraling downward through neglect. There's no holding pattern.

When I Had to Rebuild Again

After I'd rebuilt my coaching practice (after I'd cleared my Promise Debt, re-established my Protocol, and proven to myself that I could be trusted to keep commitments again) I hit a new level that exposed weaknesses I had no idea I was carrying. The practice was growing fast. Faster than I'd planned for or knew how to manage. And the me that had learned to keep promises to ten clients at a time couldn't handle the demands of twenty-five.

I was still running the same systems that worked when my client list was in its early growth stages. Client notes were getting delayed. Follow-ups were slipping. I was double-booking sessions and having to apologize. Which, given everything I'd done to build back my sense of integrity, felt like I was losing ground I'd fought hard to claim. The Protocol I'd rebuilt with so much care was cracking under the weight of complexity it was never designed to hold.

And with every broken system, every missed commitment, every moment where I couldn't deliver what I'd promised, I felt the self-trust I'd worked so hard to rebuild starting to erode again. I wasn't a failure, but I'd spiraled up to a new level that required capabilities I hadn't built yet. That distinction (between failure and underdevelopment) is one I wouldn't have been able to make a few years earlier. Back then, incompetence and inadequacy felt like the same thing. The self-reputation I'd earned around keeping individual commitments was real. That foundation was solid. What it couldn't do was automatically convert into knowing how to delegate, how to design systems for scale, or how to manage the financial complexity of a growing operation. It was the same spiral, but a whole different level. New evidence was required.

I had to admit I didn't know how to do this part, and I had to find people who did. I had to tear down systems I'd been proud of and rebuild them with more capacity. **I had to accept that being someone who had their act together in one context did not make me someone who had their act together in every context.** It was humbling. Some of it was outright humiliating, because I'd gotten comfortable with being the guy who'd figured it all out. But here I was, back to being the me that was building a coaching practice again.

I'm still in the spiral. The challenges are different now, and the stakes are different. But the pattern hasn't changed. Life keeps presenting tests that require newer forms of me. The difference is, though, I stopped fighting it. I stopped interpreting new challenges as evidence that I'd failed or that the work wasn't real. I started recognizing them for what they really are... Invitations to become someone stronger, more capable, more honest than I was the last time I got tested.

The work never ends. But the person doing the work keeps getting better at it.

What You've Actually Built

If you've done the work in this book (really fucking done it, not just read through it), you've built something foundational. But I need to be direct with you about something before we close this chapter, and in turn this book. What you've built is not a diploma. It is not a certification that you're fixed, or finished, or immune to the work that comes next. It's the base for everything still to come. One that lets you handle bigger challenges than you could before, and recover faster when those challenges knock you sideways. The confidence you've earned isn't permanent without maintenance. It's a muscle. It atrophies if you stop using it. The identity you've constructed isn't static, so it requires daily reinforcement through choices that either prove or contradict who you're becoming. The moment you treat what you've built as a trophy instead of a foundation, it starts to crack.

Life is going to test whether what you've built can hold under new pressure. It will present challenges that require capabilities you haven't developed yet. You will spiral up to levels that make you feel incompetent again. That's just how this works.

When that happens (and it will, I promise), you'll have a choice.

You can interpret the discomfort as proof that transformation is impossible, that none of this worked, that you're somehow beyond repair. You can retreat to old patterns because at least those feel familiar, and familiarity masquerades as safety.

Or you can recognize it for exactly what it is. Proof that you're growing. Proof that you're being tested at a level that matters. Proof that the foundation you've built is strong enough to support what's being constructed on top of it.

Your Next Move

This book isn't the end of your transformation. It's the end of your preparation for it. The frameworks are yours now. You built them through doing, not just reading. That's the toolkit. Now you have to use it.

Don't try to activate everything at once. That's how you build Promise Debt 2.0, by committing to ten things simultaneously and keeping none of them. Pick one area where your current identity isn't strong enough to hold what you're trying to create. Then ask yourself the questions that matter. What belief is limiting me here, and what actions and evidence will be required to build new and stronger ones? What do my hard choices reveal about my real values, and are those the values I'm trying to embody? What role am I defaulting to that isn't serving this situation?

The person you're becoming doesn't have a finish line. There's no final form that's complete and permanently adequate to handle whatever life is going to throw next. There's only the version you are today and the version your choices are building toward tomorrow.

Every kept promise is proof. Every hard choice is evidence. Every moment you show up as who you're becoming instead of defaulting to who you've been, that's a deposit into an identity that compounds over time.

The work never ends. But the person doing the work becomes someone who doesn't need it to.

CHALLENGE

Before you move forward, document what's already real.

Write down three specific areas where your behavior has changed since you started this book. Not insights. Not intentions. Actual choices you made differently, commitments you kept when you used to break them, moments where you showed up as someone you're still becoming.

For each area, answer these questions honestly. What promise did I keep that I would have abandoned three months ago? What hard choice revealed my real values when I had the option to protect a comfortable story instead? What role did I play more effectively by bringing the right energy to the right context? What belief did I replace that was quietly limiting who I thought I could become?

Now take one of those three areas and look forward. What's the next level of challenge it's preparing you for? What capability do you need to develop that doesn't exist yet? What domain is going to require new evidence, and when are you going to start building it?

Choose one commitment. Specific enough to track, daily enough to become proof, small enough that you can't negotiate your way out of it.

Then track it. Not to judge yourself. Not to feel good about your intentions. But to prove (to yourself, in the only currency that matters) that you're someone who follows through even when it costs something.

Because that's what this has always been about. Building an identity through accumulated proof that you can be trusted. Creating a self-reputation that earns access to bigger challenges. Becoming someone who doesn't need a finish line because they're too busy evolving.

The work evolves.

It never ends.

Now go build.

Epilogue: The Person Reading This No Longer Exists.

There's no going back. You can't unknow what you now know.

The person who picked up this book was searching for something they couldn't quite name. Maybe clarity about why they felt stuck despite some external successes. Or permission to want more than they were settling for. Also likely? You were tired of feeling like shit from getting pumped up by your Instagram feed and then feeling like failure when things didn't click in the real world.

That person no longer exists.

They were waiting for someone to save them. **You've learned you, and you alone, are the cavalry.** They were searching for their "true self" like it was buried treasure. You've discovered identity is built through daily choices, not unearthed through endless introspection. They thought confidence came from affirmations and believing in themselves. You know it comes from evidence, from witnessing yourself do hard things when no one's watching. They were hoping for the perfect moment to begin. You understand that clarity doesn't come *before* building, it comes *through* building. They were lying to themselves about who they are and why they're stuck. They were pointing outward for someone or something to blame. You've turned the mirror around.

You can't unknow that your life is a mirror reflecting who you've been willing to become. You can't unsee the gap between who you are and who you're capable of being. You can't unfeel the weight of Promise Debt or the emptiness of borrowed identity.

You're not the same person anymore.

The World Needs Who You're Becoming

This is the part most people miss. They treat transformation like a private project. Like something happening inside them, for them, with no particular relevance to anyone else. They journal about it. They track it. They quietly hope it sticks.

But your transformation has never been private. It has always had an audience. Not the strangers you used to stage the house for... The people who moved in.

Your kids aren't listening to what you say about discipline. They're watching whether you actually keep promises to yourself when it's inconvenient. Whether you choose hard when comfortable is available. Whether growth is something adults talk about or something adults actually do. They're learning, right now, what the relationship between effort and identity looks like in practice. You're teaching that class whether you signed up to be its teacher or not.

Your colleagues are noticing whether the changes you're making are sustainable or just another wave of temporary motivation. They're recalibrating what they believe is possible based on what you prove is possible. Not your highlights. Your consistency.

Your partner is watching whether you can admit you've been wrong, rebuild from scratch, and actually become different. That's not a small thing to witness. It either confirms their quiet belief that real change is possible, or it confirms their quiet fear that it isn't. You're writing that answer right now.

The people in your life who are still stuck (still performing, still waiting, still lying to themselves about why things haven't changed), they're watching you more closely than you know. Some of them will never say it out loud. But when you show up differently, something shifts in them. A door opens that they didn't know was there.

You won't always know who you're influencing. You won't get credit for the unspoken permission you're creating for others. But every time you choose integrity over comfort, every time you keep a promise to yourself that no one else will ever see... You're not just building yourself. You're building proof that it's possible. **And proof is the most powerful thing one human being can offer another.**

This Is Your Moment

What happens next isn't about how this book made you feel. It's not about the chapters that hit hardest or the frameworks that finally made something click or how many pages you've highlighted. Feeling moved and being changed are two different things, and you know that now.

This book can become another thing you read but didn't live. Another moment of clarity that dissolved back into the blur of old patterns and comfortable excuses. Another entry in the graveyard of good intentions. That version of this story ends with you closing the cover, feeling temporarily inspired, and slowly sliding back into the person you were before you picked it up.

Or this book becomes the line in your sand.

The moment the mirror stopped being something you avoided. When you stopped waiting for permission and started building proof. When you stopped excavating for a self that was never buried and started constructing the person capable of holding the life you actually want. When you stopped lying to yourself and started building truth. One kept promise, one hard choice, one honest decision at a time.

The person you've been can't hold what's coming. But the person you're becoming can.

So stop reading.

And start being.

Keep Building

You finished the book.

If you did the work (every challenge, every uncomfortable truth, every moment you wanted to skip and didn't) then you already know what comes next. Keep building. The work never ends. That's the point.

For everyone else...

You read the book, and somewhere between the recognition and the resistance, the work didn't happen. You read the challenges, but didn't actually put pen to paper. You nodded along with each hard truth, but kept powering through the pages.

Before you close this book, you need to decide whether you're committing to the identity change you've spent the last 200 pages reading about. Because the shelf is right there. But so is a different and much greater pathway.

If you're going to actually do this, then put skin in the game. Real accountability. Real structure. Real consequences for sliding back into the same patterns this book just named.

Most people will close this book and change nothing. Don't be most people.

Day One. 21 Days. One email a day. All implementation, no inspiration.
https://start.defytheaverage.com/day-one/

Stop Lying. Start Building. The implementation course built around Part 2.

For the person who's done the deconstruction and isn't leaving the reconstruction to chance.
https://start.defytheaverage.com/start-working/

Research Notes

I kept these out of your way while you read. No tiny numbers hovering over sentences, no footnotes breaking your stride. But some claims in this book stand on other people's work, and that work deserves naming. If you're the type who checks receipts... I like you. Here they are.

"When researchers took one of the most respected treatments for depression and stripped it down to only the behavioral part" (Introduction). Jacobson, N. S., et al. (1996). "A component analysis of cognitive-behavioral treatment for depression." Journal of Consulting and Clinical Psychology, 64(2), 295–304. The behavioral-activation component alone performed as well as the full treatment. Later work (Dimidjian et al., 2006, same journal) extended the finding.

"They call it locus of control" (Chapter 2). Julian Rotter introduced the concept in 1966 ("Generalized expectancies for internal versus external control of reinforcement," *Psychological Monographs*). Decades of research since have linked an internal locus of control to higher achievement, resilience, and wellbeing. The wheel has an academic name.

"Giving words to our feelings creates space..." (Chapter 2). Lieberman, M. D., et al. (2007). "Putting feelings into words: Affect labeling disrupts amygdala activity in response to affective stimuli." *Psychological Science*, 18(5), 421–428. Naming an emotion measurably quiets the brain's threat response. The pause has a mechanism.

"Victim, player or creator" (Chapter 2). I built this model in my own coaching practice, and learned only afterward that parts of the terrain had been mapped before. Fred Kofman's *Conscious Business* (2006) draws a victim/player line; David Emerald's *The Power of TED** (2009) works the victim-to-creator shift. I haven't read either. I list them here because their readers will recognize the neighborhood, and because an idea getting found independently more than once is usually a sign it's true.

"Measure the gain from where you started" (Chapter 5). The gap-versus-gain distinction comes from Dan Sullivan and Dr. Benjamin Hardy's *The Gap and the Gain* (2021). I use it constantly with clients because it reframes progress better than anything else I've found.

"Psychologists had people repeat 'I'm a lovable person' and measured how they felt afterward" (Chapter 6). Wood, J. V., Perunovic, W. Q. E., & Lee, J. W. (2009). "Positive self-statements: Power for some, peril for others." *Psychological Science*, 20(7), 860–866. People with low self-esteem felt worse after the affirmation. The people who need them most are the people they hurt.

"You become anxious because you've trained your brain to expect self-betrayal" (Chapter 6). This draws on Albert Bandura's research on self-efficacy, the brain's running estimate of whether you'll actually do what you set out to do. Low self-efficacy reliably tracks with higher anxiety. Your nervous system is keeping score of your follow-through whether you want it to or not.

"Psychologists call it negative reinforcement" (Chapter 8). The principle that escaping something feared produces relief, and that relief trains you to escape again, is core learning theory (O. H. Mowrer's two-factor model, 1960). It's also why exposure-based therapy, widely considered the most effective treatment for anxiety disorders, works by breaking the avoidance loop instead of feeding it. Your relief is the reward that keeps the fear alive.

"Nearly one-third of lottery winners declare bankruptcy" (the dream MINI). These figures come from financial-press reporting, not peer-reviewed research, which is why they're hedged in the text. The more famous claim (that 70 percent of winners go broke) has been disavowed by the foundation it was long attributed to. I used the conservative numbers on purpose. The argument doesn't need inflation... That's rather the point of the chapter.

"Borrowed identity becomes a form of emotional insurance" (Chapter 13). This is self-handicapping, first documented by Edward Jones and Steven Berglas (1978). People will choose obstacles or excuses in advance so that failure can be blamed on the condition rather than their own ability. Copying someone else's identity is the most comfortable handicap of all. If it doesn't work, it was never really you.

"A region of your brain, the anterior midcingulate cortex" (Chapter 14). This is genuinely new and still-developing research, popularized by neuroscientist Andrew Huberman and drawing on work by Joseph Parvizi and others on the aMCC's role in tenacity and the will to persevere. I include it because it's a striking parallel, not because it's settled. Treat it as suggestive, not proven.

"Psychologists worked it out decades ago" (Chapter 14). Bem, D. J. (1972). "Self-perception theory." In *Advances in Experimental Social Psychology*, Vol. 6. The observer in your head has an academic name and a fifty-year paper trail.

"Research shows that your brain can't tell the difference between" (Chapter 17). The suppression and surface-acting literatures, primarily Gross, J. J., & Levenson, R. W. (1997). "Hiding feelings: The acute effects of inhibiting negative and positive emotion." *Journal of Abnormal Psychology*, 106(1), 95–103, where suppressing emotion measurably increased sympathetic nervous system activation. And Hülsheger, U. R., & Schewe, A. F. (2011). "On the costs and benefits of emotional labor: A meta-analysis." *Journal of Occupational Health Psychology*, 16(3), 361–389. Performing a self you don't feel is physical work, and your body bills you for it.

About the Author

Dr. Lester Clowes is a performance and life coach with 9,000+ hours working alongside high-capacity people who've been misled by the false promises of the self-help industry. He founded DEFY after watching motivation porn pushers make big promises and collect bigger paychecks while the people who needed real change stayed stuck and grew jaded about ever changing at all. At one time, he was one of them. This book was written for everyone who will never have the chance to walk into his office, but is willing to do the work.

He lives and coaches at defytheaverage.com.

www.ingramcontent.com/pod-product-compliance
Lightning Source LLC
LaVergne TN
LVHW010552160826
845677LV00013B/3095

* 9 7 9 8 9 9 5 2 8 2 4 0 2 *